Hands-on History

American History
ACTIVITIES

Authors

Garth Sundem, M.M. and Kristi A. Pikiewicz

SHELL EDUCATION

Editor
Corinne Burton, M.A. Ed

Editorial Project Manager
Emily R. Smith, M.A. Ed.

Editor-in-Chief
Sharon Coan, M.S. Ed.

Art Director
Lee Aucoin

Imaging
Alfred Lau

Production Manager
Phil Garcia

Illustration Manager
Timothy J. Bradley

Cover Artist
Lesley Palmer

Illustrator
Timothy J. Bradley
Ana Clark

Cover Art
The Library of Congress

Standards
National Council for the Social Studies, 1994
Compendium, Copyright 2004 McREL

Publisher
Corinne Burton, M.A. Ed.

Shell Education
5301 Oceanus Drive
Huntington Beach, CA 92649-1030
http://www.shelleducation.com
ISBN 978-1-4258-0370-4
© 2005 Shell Educational Publishing, Inc.
Reprinted 2012

Table of Contents

Introduction

It was hard to carry water from the bucket to the cup at my desk because my desk was far away, and that's why people wanted to live close to rivers. Also it was easier to work as a group than on your own because you could work together and get free time for art and inventing stuff, and that's why people formed societies.

—Sixth grade student in Bozeman, Montana

Research is now validating what teachers have known intuitively all along: hands-on learning increases retention and understanding.

Using both history and political science classes, the studies found that students who participated in the role-plays and collaborative exercises did better on subsequent standard evaluations than their traditionally instructed peers (McCarthy and Anderson 2000).

For example, students at a St. Louis middle school experimenting with hands-on learning methods have scored consistently higher on the Stanford Achievement Tests than those in other district schools (Harvey, Sirna, and Houlihan 1998). In other words, once a student has built the Great Wall of China out of salt dough, he or she will remember it forever. By linking learning with experience, we encourage students to remember information as part of this action.

In addition to increasing assessment scores, hands-on learning also increases student motivation. "Tactile learning activities generated positive evaluative attitudes in fifth-grade learners toward geography. These learners did better academically when their competence was measured by content tests" (Blahut and Nicely 1984). Students enjoy hands-on activities, and when students are motivated, they learn.

Though still new to the world of social studies, hands-on learning is not revolutionary in all teaching disciplines. Science teachers use an increasingly hands-on, experimental approach in their teaching.

Introduction *(cont.)*

Jean Piaget (1986) said the following about the need for a shift toward experimental learning in science education:

> A sufficient experimental training was believed to have been provided as long as the student had been introduced to the results of past experiments or had been allowed to watch demonstration experiments conducted by his teacher, as though it were possible to sit in rows on a wharf and learn to swim merely by watching grown-up swimmers in the water . . . the repetition of past experiments is still a long way from being the best way of exciting the spirit of invention . . .

It is in hopes of exciting the spirit of invention that we offer this book of social studies simulations. More precisely, these simulations and games are designed to excite the spirit of exploration, providing both the experiential basis of knowledge and also the spark of interest so needed to encourage further study. For example, while gaining an overview of a historic period through simulated daily life, students may also be competing as small groups to conquer neighboring groups. These games are cool in much the same way that a snowball fight is cool. By making your subject cool you immediately trick students into intellectual excitement and curiosity. For many teachers in the early and middle grades, sparking this excitement in later study is a goal unto itself.

Piaget also says that involvement is the key to intellectual development. Using these games, you will involve all students, each at their differentiated level of ability and each in their preferred method of learning. For example, in the course of an activity, you may split your class into small groups in which one student makes group decisions, another interacts with neighboring groups, other students are delegated to read background material and talk with their partners, while the remaining students work to complete hands-on design and construction projects. These classroom-tested simulations involve all five of your students' senses and allow students to choose the learning styles that are best for them.

Introduction *(cont.)*

The included simulations also offer many opportunities for small group interaction, encouraging a collaborative approach to learning, which is yet another strategy validated by research. "Total reading, language, mathematics, and battery scores indicated that students in the cooperative learning class scored higher than students in the traditional class" (Pratt and Moesner 1990).

Today is an exciting time in social studies education. More and more we are creating authentic experiences for our students, be they through simulations, active learning, or even evaluation of primary source materials. We are coming to respect that it is more powerful for students to walk through the rows of crosses at Arlington National Cemetery than it is to read the words of a historian. We see that exploring African American sheet music of the 1850s as archived by the American Memory Project at the Library of Congress creates a much more personal response to segregation in American history than simply discussing the issue as a class.

We hope this book helps you infuse your classroom with the light of discovery and learning, allows you to add richness to your students' experiences, and helps you show students that history is not dead. Social studies is alive, breathing, and evolving, and not only in a laboratory or research facility, but in your classroom. People today are part of the same culture and the web of history connects us all. Through experiencing and appreciating the goals, struggles, and decisions of past societies, students in your classroom will gain a deeper appreciation for the world-changing issues facing people today.

Blahut, John M., and Robert F. Nicely Jr. 1984. Tactile activities and learning attitudes. *Social Education* 48: 153–158.

Harvey, Barbara Z.; Richard T. Sirna; Margaret B. Houlihan. 1998. Learning by design: Hands-on learning. *American School Board Journal* 186: 22–25.

McCarthy, J. Patrick and Liam Anderson. 2000. Active learning techniques versus traditional teaching styles: Two experiments from history and political science. *Innovative Higher Education* 24: 279–294.

Piaget, Jean. 1986. Essay on necessity. *Human Development* 29: 301–314.

Pratt, Sherry J. and Cheryl Moesner. 1990. A comparative study of traditional and cooperative learning on student achievement. ERIC database #325258.

How to Use This Book

Welcome to *Hands-on History: American History Activities*. Included are activities that explore eight of the topics most central to the development of the United States. While the goals of these activities are to create excitement and spark interest in further study, they are also firmly based in standards and include scoring guides and ideas for assessing student learning.

Through extensive classroom testing, we have found the best use of these activities is as an introduction to each unit. Many of the *Hands-on History* activities provide overviews in the course of role-playing activities. Students are motivated by winning a game, but they learn content-area information as a byproduct. By using these activities to prepare each unit, students come to look forward to the start of new topics and, having completed the game, will have the big picture in which to place further in-depth study. Alternately, as each unit stands alone, you can pick and choose which activities you would like to use and which you would rather leave for another year.

Be aware that some of these activities require significant preparation time. These are not everyday activities, but are the super-spectacular punctuation to which both you and your students can look forward. You will find that by organizing a general box of craft materials, you can significantly reduce the preparation time needed. You might also consider inviting motivated parents to join in the fun on activity days, adding another pair of able hands. All needed reproducibles and read-aloud directions are included within this book. So, you will find that once you organize the craft materials and form a clear picture of the game's directions in your head, the activity itself flows smoothly.

Also included are ideas for teacher-led class discussions following the National Council for History Education (NCHE) History's Habits of Mind guidelines. We have frequently found that the post-activity discussions are reason enough to run the activity, as students extend the knowledge and experience gained during the activity to make connections to the world around them. Even young students have demonstrated the understanding necessary to discuss high-level questions, learned through their own hands-on exploration of the authentic problems faced by the developing nation.

Feel free to personalize the activities, use only pieces of the activities, or expand and contract the class time as you see fit. Once you have run them a couple times, you will undoubtedly find ways to emphasize elements that fit your specific curriculum goals and will find additional discussion topics that you wish to explore. Many activities can be presented in chunks allowing you to insert materials of your choice.

In today's classrooms, teachers have to deal with the seemingly opposing forces of a recognized need for discovery-based learning and an increased desire to teach the standards. These activities can help you successfully straddle the ideological fence. Encouraging teamwork, creativity, intelligent reflection, and decision making, the activities of in this book will help you take a hands-on approach to teaching while inspiring your students to their own explorations of American history.

Overview of Activities

Colonial America (lesson on pages 11–18)

Life in Jamestown, Virginia, wasn't easy. It took hard work and smart decisions to survive. In this game-formatted activity, students will work in small groups to create their own colonies. Groups will need to manage their time and money wisely in order to complete the tasks that represent storing food and building a fort. Only the most motivated and prepared colonies will survive the winter known as the Starving Time. This game is fast-paced and fun, allowing students to make decisions and react in real time. This means that you as a teacher will want to have a firm grasp of the rules before starting the game. The total class time to complete the activity should be about three, 50-minute periods.

The American Revolution (lesson on pages 39–44)

How did this upstart nation best one of the world's most established empires? This activity explores the factors that made the American Revolution possible. This includes pressures from Napoleon, guerilla warfare, the American Indians, the Spanish, and the influence of distance. Students will divide into small groups of Patriots and British and, on a game board, will roll marbles at cardboard figures representing the other side. The first side to win a total of three battles, wins the American Revolution. Initially it looks like the British will win easily, but the game is rigged and as it progresses and outside influences come to bear, the scrappy Patriots prove to be more than the British bargained for. The total class time to complete the activity should be about two, 50-minute periods.

Jeffersonian Period (lesson on pages 51–56)

Students will role-play personalities of the Jeffersonian period and after previewing period issues using short reader's theater plays, will debate the issues in character. Character groups will vote on each issue with students earning dollars if they can successfully win others to their point of view. Following the debate, the student-characters with the most dollars will earn the right to run for president of the emerging nation, complete with campaigns and speeches. This activity previews issues and highlights the complexity of the Jeffersonian time period. The total class time to complete the activity should be about four, 50-minute periods.

Tecumseh and the American Indian Experience (lesson on pages 73–79)

Students will explore the tribal traditions, frictions, and changing ways that mark the arrival of settlers in American Indian territory. Working in small groups, students will represent American Indian tribes, the settlers of Indiana, Tecumseh, and his brother Tenskatawa. Amid simulated daily life, the two brothers will attempt to convince the tribes to unite against the influx of settlers. Unfortunately for the American Indians, the game is rigged, ending with the Battle of Tippecanoe just as alliances start to form. Students will especially appreciate the historically true ending in which an earthquake prophesied by the brothers occurs just as they said it would. But, it's too late to unite the tribes. The total class time to complete the activity should be about one to two, 50-minute periods.

Overview of Activities *(cont.)*

The Civil War *(lesson on pages 101–110)*

Though small in scale, the battle of Fayetteville, Arkansas, demonstrates the larger realities of the Civil War, as the Union First Arkansas Cavalry meets the Confederate First Arkansas Cavalry in a place both call home. Students will role-play true inhabitants of Fayetteville, working as family and neighbors to create a historically true, three-dimensional model of the town. The class will then divide into North and South and will simulate the Battle of Fayetteville, demonstrating the horrors of brothers fighting brothers as well as many of the factors, such as rifled weapons and superior tactics, that eventually led to the Union victory over the Confederates. This activity is especially successful in inspiring excitement in boys who might otherwise have little interest in the Civil War. Thanks to historian Kim Allen Scott for help in creating a historically accurate simulation. The total class time to complete the activity should be about two, 50-minute periods.

Expansion and the Oregon Trail *(lesson on pages 129–140)*

Working in small groups, students will follow the Oregon Trail from St. Louis to the rich soils of the Willamette Valley. In a choose-your-own adventure format, groups will have to make decisions along the way. Make a wrong choice and the group could be waylaid by any number of hazards. This activity explores the realities and hardships of westward expansion while providing a geographical overview of the mid-nineteenth century push toward the far coast. The total class time to complete the activity should be about three, 50-minute periods.

Immigration, Industry, and the American Dream *(lesson on pages 156–159)*

In this game, formatted as a mystery party, students will role-play representative figures of the immigration boom and second industrial revolution (1850–1920). Some, like Andrew Carnegie, are famous figures from United States history, while others will represent recent immigrants. Students have scripted questions, answers, and clues to use while trying to solve the "Mystery of the Golden Key." This fun game provides an overview of period issues and attitudes while offering students the opportunity to express their inner hams. Depending on your desired level of involvement, you can run this game with very little prep, or can have students dress up, bring food, and have a well-planned class party. The total class time to complete the activity should be about two, 50-minute periods.

Civil Rights Movement *(lesson on pages 175–178)*

Students will role-play museum curators and will explore African American art and music from before, during, and after the Harlem Renaissance. Through guided interaction with these artifacts students will experience the evolution of the African American artist from entertainer to respected member of the art community. Students will see how black pride and the Civil Rights Movement were born. The total class time to complete the activity should be about two, 50-minute periods.

Correlation to Standards

Lesson Title	NCSS Process Standard	McREL Content Standard
Colonial America	Develop empathy with the challenges faced by the earliest European Americans. (II-e)	United States History—Colonization and Settlements Standard 3—Understands why the Americas attracted Europeans, why they brought enslaved Africans to their colonies, and how Europeans struggled for control of North America and the Caribbean.
The American Revolution	Work individually and cooperatively to accomplish goals. (IV-h)	United States History—Revolution and the New Nation Standard 6—Understands the causes of the American Revolution, the ideas and interests involved in shaping the revolutionary movement, and reasons for the American victory.
Jeffersonian Period	Examine the key ideals of the democratic republican form of government such as individual liberty, justice and equality, and the rule of law. (X-a)	United States History—Expansion and Reform Standard 11—Understands the extension, restriction, and reorganization of political democracy after 1800.
Tecumseh and the American Indian Experience	Learn to empathize with both settler and the American Indian point of view. (I-b)	United States History—Expansion and Reform Standard 9—Understands the United States territorial expansion between 1801 and 1861, and how it affected relations with external powers and Native Americans.
The Civil War	Evaluate the role of physical geography in shaping human actions. (III-i)	United States History—Civil War and Reconstruction Standard 14—Understands the course and character of the Civil War and its effects on the American people.
Expansion and the Oregon Trail	Examine, interpret, and analyze physical and cultural patterns and their interactions, such as land use, settlement patterns, cultural transmission of customs and ideas, and ecosystem changes. (III-h)	United States History—Expansion and Reform Standard 10—Understands how the industrial revolution, increasing immigration, the rapid expansion of slavery, and the westward movement changed American lives and led to regional tensions.
Immigration, Industry, and the American Dream	Describe the way national/cultural roots affect individual development. (IV-c)	United States History—The Development of the Industrial United States Standard 18—Understands the rise of the American labor movement and how political issues reflected social and economic changes.
Civil Rights Movement	Identify and interpret examples of African American stereotyping and racism. (IV-g)	United States History—Postwar United States Standard 29—Understands the struggle for racial and gender equality and for the extension of civil liberties.

Colonial America

Overview

Life in Jamestown, Virginia, wasn't easy. It took hard work and smart decisions to survive. In this game-formatted activity, students will work in small groups to create their own colonies. Groups will need to manage their time and money wisely in order to complete the tasks that represent storing food and building a fort. Only the most motivated and prepared colonies will survive the winter known as the Starving Time. This game is fast-paced and fun, allowing students to make decisions and react in real time. This means that you as a teacher will want to have a firm grasp of the rules before starting the game.

The total class time to complete the activity should be about three, 50-minute periods. You will measure student learning through discussion and evaluation of game activities.

Captain John Smith
Source: Clipart.com

Objectives

- Students will develop empathy with the challenges faced by the earliest European Americans. (NCSS)
- Students will become familiar with the primary figures of early colonization and will understand the motivations that influenced formations of the first colonies.

Materials

- copies of reproducibles (pages 19–38) as described on page 12
- textbooks or other reference materials to help students answer questions on page 36
- five 9" x 12" envelopes to hold group packets
- five 24" x 24" sheets of cardboard

- extra scrap cardboard
- straw or grass
- large box of craft sticks
- clay or salt dough (recipe on page 19)
- glue
- scissors
- crayons, markers, or colored pencils

Colonial America *(cont.)*

Preparation

Preparation time should be about 30 minutes for the first day of the activity. Five to ten minutes will be needed for each additional day of the activity. (Before continuing to read this page, you may want to read the activity rules on pages 13–14 to get an overview of the whole activity.)

1. Copy and organize the materials you will need to manage the activity, including the *Jamestown Flow Sheet* (page 20) and *Easy Reference Chart* (page 21). You might consider making these sheets into overheads for easy use.

2. Create a 9" x 12" envelope packet for each group in your class (five groups total). Each packet needs to contain the following:
   - *Easy Reference Chart* (page 21)
   - *Work Hours Sheet* (page 22), cut apart
   - *Colony Information Sheet* (page 23)
   - *Task Menu* (page 24)
   - *Food Storage Sheet* (page 25)

3. Each group will also need a 24" x 24" piece of cardboard.

4. Organize a supplies table that holds all of the craft materials listed on page 11, ten copies of each *Birth Certificate* (page 26–28), five copies of each *Construction Task* (pages 29–32) descriptions, and five copies of each *Daily Task* (pages 33–36) descriptions.

5. Copy and cut apart the *Decision Cards* (page 37) and place them in a hat or box to draw from during meetings.

6. Copy and cut apart additional copies of the *Work Hours Sheet* (page 22). An extra 500 work hours per group should be adequate.

7. Make an overhead transparency of the *Habits of Mind Discussion* (page 38) to use at the conclusion of the activity.

Directions

1. In the class before the first game day, read the *Introduction Read-Aloud* (page 15).

2. Start the first actual activity day by reading the *Read-Aloud Directions* (page 16). Then, split students into five groups, distribute the envelope packets, and allow groups 5 to 10 minutes to elect a leader (John Smith) and decide which tasks they will buy with their first 500 work hours.

3. After groups purchase tasks from the teacher, begin the first season of the game. As described in depth in the *Activity Rules for the Teacher* (pages 13–14), seasons alternate with meetings. During seasons, groups will work on their tasks. During meetings, groups will get reorganized and purchase new tasks. As there are five, 15-minute seasons which alternate with five-minute meetings, you will likely need a full two class periods to organize, start, play, and complete the game.

Colonial America *(cont.)*

Directions *(cont.)*

4. Rotate through five seasons and five meetings. During each meeting time, you have to draw a *Decision Card* (page 37) for the class.

5. After the fifth season, check to see which groups have completed the necessary tasks and read the *Closure Read-Aloud* (page 17) to the students. You may reward groups that survive with a classroom privilege of your choice.

6. Use the end of the last game day or the beginning of the next class period to discuss the activity using the *Habits of Mind Discussion* (page 38) questions.

Things to Consider

1. Groups will need to elect a responsible and organized leader to act as John Smith. In order to avoid a simple popularity contest when groups vote for their leaders, be sure to emphasize the need for responsible and organized leaders.

2. In the course of the activity, settlers will die and will need to complete *Birth Certificates* (pages 26–28) in order to rejoin the game. Make sure that groups don't choose the same person to die more than once.

3. If groups fall irredeemably behind, they may lose motivation. You may want to let students know that you will display their settlements after the activity in order to keep students working toward a strong finished product.

4. Groups may sacrifice craftsmanship in favor of speed, creating a shoddy final product. Do not mark tasks as finished until students have completed them with satisfactory results.

5. If groups are off-task or unnecessarily loud at any point in the activity, you may penalize them by taking work hours.

6. If craft sticks are outside your budget, you can substitute toothpicks.

Activity Rules for the Teacher

1. Students will work in five groups representing the colony of Jamestown settlers trying to survive in the New World.

2. To survive, the group must do the following three things before the winter of 1609–1610, which was known as the Starving Time.
   - Complete the four *Construction Tasks* (pages 29–32).
   - Keep at least one settler alive at all times.
   - Complete the *Food Storage Sheet* (page 25).

3. Each group will choose a leader named John Smith who will be in charge of choosing tasks and managing the group's money, which is known as work hours.

Colonial America *(cont.)*

Activity Rules for the Teacher *(cont.)*

4. While working on *Construction Tasks*, settlers will also need to work on *Daily Tasks*, which will help them stay alive. Groups will spend any extra time on the *Food Storage Sheet*. Thus, the primary goal is to complete *Construction Tasks* and the *Food Storage Sheet*, but neglecting *Daily Tasks* might hurt the settlement.

5. The game is organized into seasons, 15 minutes used to complete tasks, called seasons, alternating with 5 minute meetings used to spend work hours, reorganize, and make decisions. As settlers arrive in 1607, there are exactly five seasons before the Starving Time and the end of the game.

6. Each group starts with 500 work hours, which they will use during the first meeting to buy tasks at the cost of 300 work hours per *Construction Task* and 150 work hours per *Daily Task*. During each meeting, groups will receive another 500 work hours.

7. When a season starts, each group will send a representative to the crafts table where he or she will find the information sheets describing the task the group has purchased as well as all materials needed to complete the task. Each group will try to complete its task before the end of the season. If a group fails to finish the task in the course of one season, the group will need to use more work hours to purchase the task again.

8. Keep track of purchased and completed tasks on the *Jamestown Flow Sheet* (page 20).

9. In each meeting, you will:

   • give each group another 500 work hours.

   • ask each John Smith which task his or her group completed and mark the *Jamestown Flow Sheet*.

   • draw a *Decision Card* (page 37). If a decision is required, ask each group to decide and then assign consequences according to directions on the card. In this step, settlers may die.

   • collect work hours from the John Smiths to purchase new tasks or repurchase any unfinished tasks from the previous season. Once a task is purchased, mark a W for work in progress on the *Jamestown Flow Sheet*. When a task is finished, mark an F.

10. If for any reason a group cannot pay needed work hours, one settler will die. Groups will choose who dies, but everyone must die once before they may repeat.

11. If a settler dies, he or she will need to complete a *Birth Certificate* in order to rejoin the game. Quickly jot down who dies, give him or her a *Birth Certificate*, and then mark him or her alive once they complete the *Birth Certificate*.

12. Once settlers have filled their silo on the *Food Storage Sheet*, they may trade extra food for additional work hours.

Teacher Note: For a concise description of the parts of the game for students, see the *Easy Reference Chart* (page 21).

Colonial America *(cont.)*

Introduction Read-Aloud

You may have heard of Christopher Columbus and his ships, the *Niña*, *Pinta*, and *Santa Maria*. You might remember hearing something about the *Mayflower* that brought the first Pilgrims to the Plymouth Bay Colony looking for religious freedom. It all had something to do with turkeys, cranberry sauce, and funny hats, right? In fact, the first successful colony of British settlers in the New World landed in Virginia more than 100 years after Columbus and almost 15 years before the Pilgrims.

The year was 1607 and a business called the London Company sent a group of gentlemen explorers to the New World hoping to find a way to make money. Their first choice was to find a river that would provide easy travel across the continent so that ships could go straight through to China and the East. Their second choice was to stumble onto a huge pile of gold and become fabulously rich. When neither of these things happened, the going got rough for the gentlemen explorers. It was a good thing one of them was not much of a gentleman.

John Smith was an explorer. He had fought Turks in Hungary, been a slave in Constantinople, wandered through Russia, and fought pirates in North Africa all before he was 28 years old. The rest of the men kept Smith locked in chains below deck for most of the sea voyage. They thought he was an uncultured braggart; but when the going got rough, they recognized that John Smith was their only chance for survival.

When the gentlemen in the colony did not want to work, John Smith said that was okay, but they also would not get to eat. As you can guess, the gentlemen decided to work.

Even so, the settlers had to deal with disease, unstable relations with the American Indians, harsh winters, and inexperience with the kinds of hunting and planting necessary to survive.

So, what happened to the settlers in Jamestown? Do you think that under John Smith's leadership the colony was able to survive? Do you think life suddenly got easy and the settlers got fat eating pumpkin pie? We'll see . . .

Tomorrow we will break into small groups. You will elect a leader and through hard work and good decisions you will try to create your own settlement in Jamestown. With a little luck you might even survive in the New World!

Colonial America *(cont.)*

Read-Aloud Directions

Your group of settlers has been sent to Virginia by the London Company. You will need to create a colony capable of surviving the harsh climate and the sometimes unfriendly American Indians.

Each group has an envelope from the London Company, which you will open when we start the game. Included in the envelope are all the directions you will need. We will also go over the directions now.

1. Your goal is to survive. To survive, you will need to do three things. Complete the *Construction Tasks*, complete the *Food Storage Sheet*, and have at least one person stay alive at all times.

2. There are also *Daily Tasks*. While your goal is to finish the *Construction Tasks*, don't forget about the *Daily Tasks* or you might not survive long enough to build anything.

3. There will be seasons and meetings. During seasons, you will work on the tasks. During meetings you will decide which tasks to work on, make decisions, and get reorganized.

4. Tasks cost money. During each meeting, you will choose how to spend your money, called work hours.

5. When you buy a task, I will mark that you are working. When you finish, show me your completed task and I will mark the task completed. If you don't finish a task during one season, you will need to spend work hours to buy the task again.

6. You will elect a leader, named John Smith, who will make most of the decisions for your group.

7. During the game, settlers may die. If you die, you will need to complete a *Birth Certificate* before you can rejoin the game.

8. Try to stay on task and don't speak out of turn during the activities or you may be penalized work hours.

9. Remember your goals: *Construction Tasks, Food Storage Sheet,* and stay alive. Your John Smith will manage your work hours and decide which tasks to buy. The rest of the group will work on completing tasks as quickly as possible during the seasons.

Colonial America (cont.)

Closure Read-Aloud

Though the first five seasons were hard for the Jamestown settlers, they were nothing compared to the winter of 1609–1610. So what was the big deal? Why was this winter so much harder than all the others?

The settlers prepared for the winter just like any other. They stocked food in the storehouse including corn and vegetables, had pigs and goats, as well as chickens that provided eggs and meat. All the settlers had to do to get food was head into the nearby forest where they could hunt deer and rabbits and fish in the waters that almost surrounded the settlement. Most of the settlers' problems up until this point had been with disease and, every once in a while, with American Indians. Food was not much of a concern.

But what would happen if the settlers were all of a sudden unable to go into the forest to hunt? What would happen if they couldn't get to the waters to fish? In fact, do you think the settlers could survive if they weren't even able to go outside their own colony's walls? Well, that's what happened in 1609 when American Indians laid siege to the Jamestown settlement. With their town surrounded, the settlers had to survive the winter eating only what was stored inside the walls. How did your settlements do?

Answer Key

Below are the answers to the student task activity sheets (pages 25–36).

Food Storage Sheet (page 25)

1. c
2. b
3. a
4. d
5. c
6. a

7. Here are a few short definitions you can use to check student work.

   Pilgrim—religious people who founded the colony in Plymouth

   yeoman—a farmer who cultivates his own land

   palisade—a fence forming a fortification around a settlement

   wattle and dub—building material consisting of mud and twigs

   treaty—a formal agreement between groups of people

8. Columbus = 1, Massachusetts Pilgrims = 3, Jamestown Settlers = 2

Colonial America *(cont.)*

Answer Key *(cont.)*

Birth Certificate I (page 26)

Check to make sure the student-drawn pictures are done with care and represent the listed items.

Birth Certificate II (page 27)

Check for a short description written from the American Indian perspective.

Birth Certificate III (page 28)

1. John Smith 2. Virginia 3. Plymouth 4. Explore; The clues should spell "iron pyrite." The extra credit question is "fool's gold."

Palisade (page 29)

Students should have craft sticks stuck vertically in cardboard forming a wall around the settlement.

Houses (page 30)

Students should have one house per group member made of craft sticks and covered in salt dough or clay.

Church (page 31)

Made of craft sticks and salt dough or clay, churches should be two stick lengths long, one stick length wide, and at least three inches tall. It must have a sloped roof.

Cannon (page 32)

This is a rolled tube of paper with toothpick and cardboard wheels as shown.

Hunt (page 33)

Students should have circled the six listed animals in the picture and provided short, thoughtful answers to the questions that follow.

Farm (page 34)

Students should have illustrated the four farming techniques to the best of their abilities.

Explore (page 35)

Students should have circled England, Virginia, and China on the first map and drawn routes around the southern tip of Africa and across the United States. On the back, students should have illustrated a map of Virginia showing Chesapeake Bay, the James River, and Jamestown.

Dig a Well (page 36)

1. b   3. d
2. a   4. a

Recipe for Salt Dough

Ingredients

4 cups flour

1 cup salt

1½ cups hot water (from tap)

2 teaspoons vegetable oil (optional)

Directions

Mix the salt and flour together, then gradually add the water until the dough becomes elastic. Add two teaspoons of vegetable oil at this point. If your mixture turns out too sticky, simply add more flour. If it turns out too crumbly, add more water. Knead the dough until it's a good consistency.

You can store your salt dough in a sealed container in the refrigerator, but it will not usually last more than a couple of days.

Jamestown Flow Sheet

Mark "W" for working or "F" for finished

			Summer 1607	Winter 1607–08	Summer 1608	Winter 1608–09	Summer 1609
Group 1	Construction	palisade					
		houses					
		church					
		cannon					
	Daily	hunt					
		farm					
		explore					
		dig well					
Group 2	Construction	palisade					
		houses					
		church					
		cannon					
	Daily	hunt					
		farm					
		explore					
		dig well					
Group 3	Construction	palisade					
		houses					
		church					
		cannon					
	Daily	hunt					
		farm					
		explore					
		dig well					
Group 4	Construction	palisade					
		houses					
		church					
		cannon					
	Daily	hunt					
		farm					
		explore					
		dig well					
Group 5	Construction	palisade					
		houses					
		church					
		cannon					
	Daily	hunt					
		farm					
		explore					
		dig well					

Easy Reference Chart

During Meetings (Mostly John Smiths)	During Seasons (Mostly other than John Smith)
• Groups STOP working on their *Construction Tasks, Daily Tasks,* or *Food Storage Sheet.* • Teacher will give each group 500 more work hours. • Teacher draws, reads, and collects on a *Decision Card.* • John Smiths purchase *Construction Tasks* for 300 work hours and *Daily Tasks* for 150 work hours for the next season. • Teacher marks "W" for work in progress or "F" for finished on the *Jamestown Flow Sheet.*	• Groups work on *Construction Tasks, Daily Tasks,* and the *Food Storage Sheet.* • John Smiths may help, manage, or choose in advance the tasks they will purchase during the next meeting.

Remember groups may be penalized work hours for any off-task behavior. At the end of the class period, gather all your work hours and excess materials in your group envelope and put them away for the next day.

Jamestown Map

Work Hours Sheet

Directions: Cut along the dotted lines before distributing these to students.

Colony Information Sheet

Welcome to Jamestown, Virginia. You will be working as a group to create a settlement.

1. Your first task is to elect a leader, named John Smith. Your John Smith will be in charge of managing the group's money and making decisions. He or she will need to be responsible and organized. Elect a John Smith **now**.

2. Now that you have a John Smith, you will decide how to spend your first 500 work hours. The goal of the game is to complete the four *Construction Tasks* and to finish the *Food Storage Sheet*. But do not neglect the *Daily Tasks* or you might not survive long enough to construct anything!

   • *Construction Tasks* cost 300 work hours each.

   • *Daily Tasks* cost 150 work hours each.

   Now, take a look at the *Task Menu* and decide how you will spend your first 500 work hours.

3. Remember, your John Smith will make decisions and take charge of your work hours. Everyone else will try to complete the tasks as quickly as possible during the seasons of the game. If you don't complete a task during one season, you have to pay for it again.

   You only have five seasons to work on your tasks before the Starving Time! Good luck.

Task Menu

Construction Tasks
300 work hours each

Palisade

Before airplanes, a small wall was a strong protection against attack. A palisade is like a strong fence made of pointed logs. Build a palisade around your settlement.

Houses

Without a roof over your head, there would be no hope of surviving the harsh winters. You will need to build a house for each member of your colony.

Church

Though the colony at Jamestown wasn't a group of religious pilgrims, life still revolved around the church. The church served as a meeting hall and social center. Build a church to hold your community together.

Cannon

Flying metal balls were not the only damage cannons inflicted. The explosions and flashes from cannons were effective psychological weapons as well. Build a cannon to protect your settlement.

Daily Tasks
150 work hours each

Hunt

The forest around your settlement is full of wild game, but it will take intelligence and skill to store food for the winter. Hunt for food to keep your settlement satisfied.

Farm

Inch by inch, row by row, you had better make a garden grow, but it might take a little more than a rake and a hoe to learn the farming techniques that work in the New World.

Explore

According to the London Company, part of the settlers' job was to explore and map the New World. Exploration helped settlers locate sources of food and resources, and allowed them to set up trade with American Indians. Explore the area around your settlement.

Dig a Well

Finding clean drinking water was a problem in Jamestown. Dig a well to avoid getting sick.

Names _____

Food Storage Sheet

Directions: Complete this sheet to store food for the Starving Time. You may need to look for answers in your textbook. When you finish, show this sheet to your teacher. For every correct answer you will gain one week of provisions. Mark your provisions by coloring the silo. If you have extra food, you can trade it for work hours (1 week = 100 work hours). If you do not have at least eight correct answers, you will have to do more research in order to make it through the Starving Time.

1. The first permanent settlement in Virginia was known as:

    a. Abbottsville   b. Plymouth   c. Jamestown   d. Bay Colony

2. The American Indian who saved John Smith's life was named:

    a. Powhatan   b. Pocahontas   c. Algonquin   d. Tecumseh

3. The first European settlers came to Virginia to:

    a. make money   c. meet American Indians

    b. find religious freedom   d. grow cotton

4. The company that sent the first settlers to Virginia was known as the:

    a. Chesapeake Bay Company   c. Spain Company

    b. England Company   d. London Company

5. Settlers first came to Jamestown in:

    a. 1492   b. 1512   c. 1607   d. 1776

6. The Jamestown settlement was named after the:

    a. king of Great Britain   c. pope

    b. mayor of New York   d. king of Spain

7. Write short definitions of the following terms:

    • Pilgrim: _____

    • yeoman: _____

    • palisade: _____

    • wattle and daub: _____

    • treaty: _____

8. Rank the following people or groups from 1–3, ordering their visits to the New World.

    _____ Columbus   _____ Massachusetts Pilgrims _____ Jamestown Settlers

Name _____

Birth Certificate I

You are dead! Complete this sheet to rejoin the game. Show your teacher when you are done.

The settlers' relationship with the American Indians was sometimes good and sometimes bad. Sometimes they traded and sometimes they fought. Often the most difficult part was communication.

Directions: The tables below show English words and their Algonquin translations. Draw a picture under each set of words that both groups would be able to recognize. If your teacher thinks your drawings are unclear, you will have to work a little harder in order to be reborn into the colony.

corn madamin	shirt pabagiwayan	milk toodoshanabo	bread pakwejigan

meat wiyas	food midjin	horse pepejigogashkwe	wolf maigan

Name _____

Birth Certificate II

You are dead! Complete this sheet to rejoin the game. Show your teacher when you are done.

Much of what we hear from the settlers describes the American Indians as uneducated savages with strange traditions. What do you think the American Indians thought of the settlers? Do you think the American Indians thought the settlers were just as weird?

Directions: Rewrite the italicized passage below as if you are an American Indian. Be creative! What would you have seen? What would you think of the settlers? When you are finished, show your teacher in order to be reborn into the colony.

> *"Indians came creeping upon all fours . . . like bears, with the bows in their mouths, but when they felt the sharpness of our shot, they retired into the woods with great noise."*
>
> —*George Percy, British gentleman*

_____

_____

_____

_____

_____

_____

_____

_____

Name _____

Birth Certificate III

You are dead! Complete this sheet to rejoin the game. Show your teacher when you are done.

The settlers who landed in Jamestown thought they would find gold lying on the beaches and life would be easy. In fact, their captain, Christopher Newport, gathered a whole barrel of shiny metal and returned to England.

Directions: Answer the questions below to decode the message and discover what it was that Newport brought back to England.

1. What was the name of the most successful Jamestown leader?

    ___ ___ ___ ___   ___ ___ ___ ___ ___
        1   2   3   4

2. Jamestown was in which colony?

    ___ ___ ___ ___ ___ ___ ___ ___ ___
        5   6

3. What was the name of the famous rock where the Pilgrims landed?

    ___ ___ ___ ___ ___ ___ ___ ___ ___
    7   8

4. The settlers of Jamestown sent men to _____ the James River looking
    for the Inside Passage.

    ___ ___ ___ ___ ___ ___ ___
    9   10

Write the letters from the clues above the correct numbers:

3	6	1	2		7	8	10	5	4	9

Extra credit:

Do you know another name for this substance?

    ___ ___ ___ ___ ___ ,   ___ ___ ___ ___ ___

Palisade Construction Task

If this is your first *Construction Task*, get a piece of cardboard large enough to be the base of your model settlement.

Directions: A palisade is a wall made of pointy logs that surrounds a settlement. It is a strong form of defense against enemies. This is a difficult task to complete in one 15-minute season, so you need to work quickly!

- Draw a triangle on your cardboard that is big enough to fit houses, a church, and cannons inside. This is the outline of your palisade wall.

- Make a four-inch tall wall that sits on your triangular outline. Vertically stick craft sticks into the cardboard base to create this wall. Glue your wall in place and prop it up with more craft sticks if needed.

- Glue straw or grass on the outside of your wall. It should look like your palisade wall is made of many logs stuck into the ground.

This is what a palisade looks like from the inside.
You will only be creating the palisade and not the tower or walkway.

Houses Construction Task

If this is your first *Construction Task*, get a piece of cardboard large enough to be the base of your model settlement.

Directions: Houses in the Jamestown settlement were made of wattle and daub, which is sticks and clay. Use craft sticks and glue to make a log cabin style house for each of the members of your settlement, including your John Smith. Once you have made log cabin frames, cover them with clay or salt dough and place them inside your settlement. Houses need to be at least two inches tall.

This is what a wattle and daub house looks like.

Church Construction Task

If this is your first *Construction Task*, get a piece of cardboard large enough to be the base of your model settlement.

A church might not seem like such an important building to a group of people who came to the New World looking for fame and fortune, but the church at Jamestown was not only a place of worship, it was also the settlement's meeting area and social center. The church was a combination of church and town hall.

Directions: Use craft sticks and glue to build a church for your settlement. It needs to be at least two stick lengths long, one stick length wide, and three inches tall. Once you have made a log cabin frame, cover it with clay or salt dough. Do not forget to make a sloping roof (not flat!) or else water will sit on the top of your church and it will rot during the first winter.

This is the church at Jamestown.

Cannon Construction Task

If this is your first *Construction Task*, get a piece of cardboard large enough to be the base of your model settlement.

Cannons were the most powerful weapons in the New World. In addition to the damage they caused, they also made a huge flash and a loud bang. Even if enemies were not killed, just seeing a cannon go off was sometimes enough to frighten away attackers.

Directions:

1. Cut out the cannon template below.
2. Roll it into a tube and tape or glue it shut.
3. Poke a toothpick through your tube through the two circles.

4. Cut out the wheels.
5. Glue them to the base of the cannon.
6. Decorate your cannon.

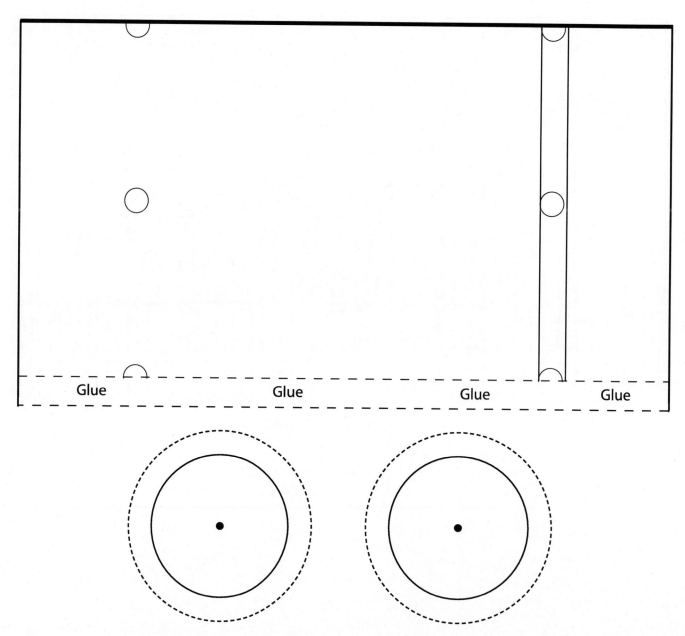

Hunt Daily Task

Directions: Look at the picture below. Find, circle, and label the following animals: turkey, deer, boar (wild pig), bear, bison, and duck.

The American Indian hunters used controlled burns to clear the underbrush away from the woods surrounding their villages, while leaving the trees standing. With this in mind, answer the following questions (if you need extra space, use the back of this sheet).

1. How would burning the underbrush affect finding animals?

   _____

   _____

2. How would burning the underbrush affect travel by foot in the forest?

   _____

   _____

3. How would burning the underbrush affect a tribe's defense?

   _____

   _____

4. How would burning the underbrush affect fleas, bugs, and rodents?

   _____

   _____

Farm Daily Task

The American Indians farmed using techniques they had developed over hundreds of years to fit the needs of the land. When the settlers arrived, they used their European farming methods, which did not work nearly as well.

Directions: Below, draw pictures to illustrate each of the following American Indian farming practices. Your pictures need to be good enough so that your teacher can tell which technique they are supposed to represent.

1. American Indians relied on wild crops such as chestnuts, acorns, hickory nuts, blueberries, strawberries, fruit trees, and edible roots, which they gathered as a tribe.

2. Instead of clearing land for crops, American Indians just expanded existing clearings in the forest. After killing only the first layer of trees, they would burn the clearing underbrush and work the ashes into the soil to provide fertilizer for their crops.

3. American Indians planted many crops together, instead of putting only one type of crop in a field. By planting corn, beans, and squash together, the beans helped put needed nitrogen in the soil, the corn provided poles for the beans to climb, and the big squash leaves shaded the ground and kept weeds from growing.

4. After 15 years, the nutrients in the soil were mostly used up, so American Indians let the field return to natural woodland.

1.	2.
3.	4.

Explore Daily Task

The London Company, the company that sent the settlers to Jamestown wanted to find gold. They also wanted to find a river that went across the New World so that they could easily get from England to the East. Though it had not yet been found, they called this river the Inside Passage.

Directions: Circle England, Virginia, and China on the map below. Draw the route that a boat has to travel to get from England to China. Now, pretend that a boat could go straight across the U.S. Draw the route you could take to get from England to China. This is the Inside Passage that everybody was trying to find.

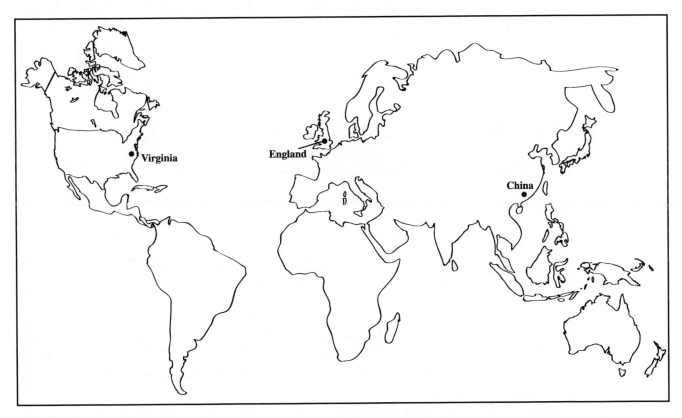

In your textbook or on a map, find Virginia. Find the Chesapeake Bay, and then find the James River. The settlement of Jamestown was on the James River. On the back of this page, draw a map of eastern Virginia showing the following things:

• Chesapeake Bay

• The James River

• Jamestown Settlement

Dig a Well Daily Task

Finding clean water was a major problem for the early settlers of Jamestown. Without it, many people died of a horrible disease called dysentery. The drawing below is what the ground looked like in Jamestown. There is lots of water on the surface, but it is all swampy and mucky, full of mosquito eggs and bad bacteria. Like most places, there is also a lot of water underground. The further down you dig, the wetter the soil becomes. If you dig a hole into this wet soil, the hole will fill in with water. That makes a well!

Directions: Look in your textbook or other resource available in your classroom to find answers to the following disease questions. Using each book's index to look up terms will save you some time. For each correct question, you can dig five feet down. You have to dig at least 20 feet to get to the clean water.

1. The disease that settlers got from unclean water was:

   a. smallpox   b. dysentery   c. typhoid   d. scurvy

2. The disease that American Indians got from settlers, eventually killing a huge percentage of the population was:

   a. smallpox   b. dysentery   c. typhoid   d. scurvy

3. The disease that sailors got from lack of vitamin C (no fruit) that made their teeth fall out was:

   a. smallpox   b. dysentery   c. typhoid   d. scurvy

4. The disease that leaves pockmark scars on the face and body:

   a. smallpox   b. dysentery   c. typhoid   d. scurvy

Decision Cards

Directions: Copy and cut these cards for the activity. Draw one card for the whole class during each meeting.

Decision If you have not completed digging a well, your settlement is without clean water and one member dies of dysentery.	**Decision** Do you trust the American Indian Pocahontas? **Yes** = group remains the same **No** = John Smith dies
Decision If you have not completed farming then one of your settlers starves to death.	**Decision** Are you more concerned about disease or being attack by American Indians? **Disease** = group remains same **American Indians** = one settler dies of typhoid fever
Decision If you have not completed exploration, then one of your settlers gets lost while hunting and dies.	**Decision** Do you use English or American Indian farming techniques? **Indian** = group remains same **English** = one settler starves to death
Decision If you have not completed hunting, then one of your settlers starves to death.	**Decision** Do you settle on land with good natural defenses even though the ground is swampy? **Yes** = one settler dies of malaria **No** = group remains same

Habits of Mind Discussion

- What do you think was the biggest danger to early settlers in the New World?

- Do you think that American Indians or settlers got the worst of the "disease exchange"?

- What could the London Company have done differently to help the Jamestown settlers succeed?

- What could the settlers have done to help themselves succeed?

- What do you think would have happened to the settlers without the leadership of John Smith? Why?

- What would have happened if the Jamestown settlers had not survived the Starving Time? How would the United States be different today?

The American Revolution

Overview

How did this upstart nation best one of the world's most established empires? This activity explores the factors that made the American Revolution possible. This includes pressures from Napoleon, guerilla warfare, the American Indians, the Spanish, and the influence of distance. Students will divide into small groups of Patriots and British and, on a game board, will roll marbles at cardboard figures representing the other side. The first side to win a total of four battles, wins the American Revolution. Initially it looks like the British will win easily, but the game is rigged and as it progresses and outside influences come to bear, the scrappy Patriots prove to be more than the British bargained for.

The total class time to complete the activity should be about two, 50-minute periods. You will measure student learning through discussion and evaluation of game activities.

Surrender at Saratoga
Source: The Library of Congress

Objectives

- Students will work individually and cooperatively to accomplish goals. (NCSS)
- Students will understand the factors that contributed to the victory of the Patriots over the British in the American Revolution.

Materials

- copies of reproducibles (pages 45–50) as described on page 40
- one large marble per group (4 to 6 groups)
- scissors
- tape

- crayons, markers, or colored pencils
- two or three pieces of 11" x 17" poster board or construction paper for the game boards
- five 9" x 12" envelopes to hold group packets

The American Revolution *(cont.)*

Preparation

Total preparation time should be around 10 minutes. Ask a parent to volunteer to help with the copying before you begin the activity.

1. Create a 9" x 12" envelope packet for each group in your class (groups of four or six). Each packet needs to contain the following:
   * *American Revolution Game Rules* (page 45)
   * *Materials Instruction Sheet* (page 46)
   * *British Soldier Template* (page 47) enough for five soldiers per student on each British team
   * *Patriot Soldier Template* (page 48) enough for three soldiers per student on each Patriot team
   * *Weapon Ramp Template* (page 49), copy on cardboard if possible

2. Cut 11" x 17" pieces of poster board or construction paper (one per group) for students to make their game boards.

3. Divide your class into groups of four or six. This will put an even number of British and Patriots in each group. If you have an odd number of students, one or more groups will have to have students play multiple roles.

4. Make an overhead transparency of the *Habits of Mind Discussion* (page 50) to use at the conclusion of the activity.

Directions

1. Read the *Introduction Read-Aloud* (page 41) to the students. Follow the teacher notes within the introduction to get the class ready to begin the activity.

2. Once students have created their game materials, read the *Read-Aloud Directions* (page 42).

3. Then, read the "Before the Game" directions from the *Battle One Description: Long Island* (page 42). Pass out one marble to each group, and let students play to a conclusion according to the game rules.

4. Once all groups are done, chart how many British and how many Patriots won their small-group battles. The side with the most small-group wins is victorious in the overall battle. The British will likely win this first battle easily. Read the "After the Game" comments from the *Battle One Description: Long Island* (page 42).

5. Repeat the above technique with the *Battle Two Description: Princeton* (page 42), *Battle Three Description: Fort Edward* (page 43), and the rest of the battle descriptions until one side has won a total of four battles. The game is rigged such that the Patriots should win after 6–7 total battles.

6. Read the *Closure Read-Aloud* (page 44) to the students.

7. Clean up the game materials and finish with the *Habits of Mind Discussion* (page 50). Depending on the efficiency of your class, you may complete the entire game in one period, following with the discussion at the beginning of the next period. Or, you may need to continue the game itself into a second period, finishing with the discussion at the end of this period.

The American Revolution *(cont.)*

Things to Consider

1. As this is a game of chance and skill, there is a slight possibility that even though the game is heavily rigged, the British will, in fact, win. If this happens, you will want to discuss the overwhelming odds the Patriots faced and reinforce the role of luck in helping the Patriots triumph over the British. Help students see that this conflict could easily have ended with a Patriots loss. How would the world be different today?

2. Clean-up time and time to reset the activity are required at the end of the game period. Take this into account when scheduling, especially if you are a single-subject teacher, using the activity in back-to-back classes; you may need to run the activity on different days for different periods.

Introduction Read-Aloud

"The British are coming! The British are coming!" Even though Paul Revere didn't really say this, it sure is a catchy phrase.

In 1775, the world's most powerful fighting force landed in New York to put down a rebellion of poorly equipped, underpaid, untrained Patriots. It looked like an easy task for the mighty British Empire, who intimidated the world with their tight-marching columns of trained soldiers, bright red uniforms, and rows of bayonets fixed on the ends of their weapons. To the British, this was a chance to teach the upstart Patriots a quick lesson before returning to business as usual with their many colonies.

To the Patriots it was a bit more.

We will be forming groups of British and Patriots and will be replaying some of the battles of the American Revolution. While we all know who won in real life, this one is up for grabs. It will take skill and a little bit of luck to triumph in this, the New World!

Teacher note: Place students into groups of four or six. Within each group, have them divide in half into a British and a Patriot sub-group.

Now we will create the three things each group needs to play the game: soldiers, a game board, and a weapon ramp. You have ten minutes to create these three things. All the directions you need are included on the activity sheets I am passing out.

Teacher note: Pass out the envelopes with reproducibles that you prepared based on the directions on page 40. Also give each group a piece of 11" x 17" paper for the game board and allow ten minutes for completion.

The American Revolution *(cont.)*

Read-Aloud Directions

Okay, now that we all have our game materials, it is time to play. Here are the rules:

1. In each group, you will be fighting a series of battles between the British and the Patriots. In each battle, the side with the most small-group wins will be victorious in the overall battle. The first side to win four battles wins the war.

2. Before each battle, I will read a short description that might change the rules slightly, so listen carefully. But generally, you will be lining up your paper figures and taking turns rolling a marble down the weapon ramp, trying to knock over the other side's soldiers. Once a side has knocked down all the opposing soldiers, the battle is over.

3. You will take turns rolling. You will get one roll per soldier you still have standing. For example, if three of your original British soldiers are still upright, you will get three rolls before it is the other team's turn.

4. Unless the battle description says otherwise, you need to roll at the other team's soldiers from behind the middle line, though you may move the weapon ramp anywhere you like behind the line.

5. Each British student will start with five soldiers, and each Patriot student will start with three soldiers. Once a soldier falls, you will remove him from the board.

6. You may not push the marble down the weapon ramp. You must set it at the top and then let it roll on its own. Please try to keep the marbles from hitting the floor.

Battle One Description: Long Island

Before the Game: General Washington and his small group of Patriots meet Sir William Howe and the British army on Long Island. *Both the British and the Patriots need to position their people in the game area marked "A."*

After the Game: The Patriots are routed, but luckily General Washington retreats before losing his entire army. Aided by a thick fog, the Patriots retreat across the Delaware River and are pushed all the way to Pennsylvania where the British cease their chase due to the onset of winter.

Battle Two Description: Princeton

Before the Game: Washington and the Patriots leave a few soldiers to keep their campfires burning and sneak into Princeton, New Jersey, catching the British off guard. *Each Patriot gets a free roll from the zone marked "D" before the game starts. Both sides start with troops in their areas marked "A."*

After the Game: Though not a huge victory, the Patriots show they can fight the British and win. The triumph in Princeton, New Jersey, wins many new recruits to the Patriot cause.

The American Revolution *(cont.)*

Battle Three Description: Fort Edward

Before the Game: British General John Burgoyne marches into Fort Edward, but where are the Patriots? They have fled the fort, but have left logs covering the road, making it difficult for the British to transport their heavy cannons and wagons. With the British stuck on the road, the Patriots shoot at them from the woods. *The Patriots may place two pencils anywhere they like on the game board, and may fire from the areas marked "E."*

After the Game: Fort Edward is a strong victory for the Patriots and demonstrates the effectiveness of guerilla warfare.

Battle Four Description: Cornwallis in the South

Before the Game: A new general is in charge of the British army. Lord Charles Cornwallis sails south from New York into Georgia. The British depend on their superior cannon power. *The British may roll crumpled paper down the weapon ramp with their marbles. They may shoot from the area marked "C."*

After the Game: Cornwallis sweeps through Savannah, Georgia, Charleston, South Carolina, and Camden, South Carolina, handing the Patriots devastating losses.

Battle Five Description: Saratoga

Before the Game: Patriot General Horatio Gates sets up cannons on a bluff to guard a small stretch of road below. Instead of walking the dangerous road, General Burgoyne decides to fight the dug-in Patriots on the bluff. Unfortunately for Burgoyne, American farmers join the battle, bringing with them their deadly accurate rifles. *To symbolize increased accuracy, the Patriots may push the marble (not too hard!) instead of just rolling it down the ramp and may shoot from the area marked "D."*

After the Game: The Battle of Saratoga was a great victory for the Patriots; due mainly to the accuracy of the farmers' rifles and the readiness of the Patriot defenses. The British lost 600 soldiers to the Patriot's 150.

Battle Six Description: Vincennes

Before the Game: At the battle of Vincennes, the Patriots are led by General George Rogers Clark. They attack a British fort that is fortified with many cannons. While this does not sound like such a good idea, General Clark has a plan. He keeps his troops moving at all times so they cannot be hit by cannons, and he has them whoop and shout to make the British inside the fort think there are many more attackers than there actually are. *In this battle, the British must shoot cannons (wadded balls of paper) instead of muskets (marbles), stay behind the center line, and set up troops only in their area "A." The Patriots may reposition their troops after every roll into areas "A" or "B."*

The American Revolution *(cont.)*

Battle Six Description: Vincennes *(cont.)*

After the Game: To the British inside Fort Vincennes, it sounded like they were being attacked by an army of thousands, but this army would not stand still. The British could not hit them with their cannons. In fact, General Clark had only 150 men with him. The British fort surrendered.

Battle Seven Description: Yorktown

Before the Game: In August 1781, British General Cornwallis marches his troops to Yorktown, a river port on the Chesapeake Bay in Virginia. Unfortunately for Cornwallis, the French had joined the war on the side of the Patriots. Cornwallis depends on being able to get supplies from fleets of British ships, but French Admiral Comte de Grasse stops these ships from reaching Yorktown. General Washington sets up a horseshoe of troops around the British on land, who are backed against the water. *In this battle, both Patriots and British may shoot cannons (crumpled paper balls) instead of muskets (marbles) if they choose. Patriots may fire from the game board areas marked "E," while the British must stay behind the center line.* This battle was also influenced by a daring raid led by Alexander Hamilton. *At any point you choose, a Patriot may fire two extra cannon balls from the area marked "F." British must line up in area "A," while the Patriots can line up in "A" or "B."*

After the Game: Yorktown was the last battle of the American Revolution. On October 17, 1781, a British officer climbed out of the trenches waving a white handkerchief. The Patriots were victorious.

Closure Read-Aloud

So what do you think? Was the game fair? Of course, it wasn't fair! The Patriots cheated! But have you ever heard the quote, "All's fair in love and war"? Maybe the British should have paid a little more attention when they learned this quote in school.

After the first couple of disastrous battles, the Patriots learned to break all the established rules of warfare. Much to the dismay of the British they wouldn't stand still in the middle of an open field wearing bright coats that looked like big red bull's-eyes. And, they used resources, like sharp-shooting farmers the British had never counted on. The Patriots learned from their mistakes and made up their strategies as they went, without hundreds of years of military tradition telling them what to do. They were able to adapt to the land and to the changing circumstances of each battle. Which British general would have thought to run around in circles yelling, like Clark? And which British leader would have left fires burning to trick the enemy, like Washington at Princeton?

These Patriots, through their creativity and resourcefulness, were able to best one of the mightiest empires in the world, while laying the principles of courage and individualism on which the American ideal was founded.

American Revolution Game Rules

1. You are fighting battles between the Patriots and the British.

2. To win, you need to knock over all the opposing side's soldiers by rolling a marble down your weapon ramp.

3. You need to roll from your own side of the centerline.

4. Each student gets one roll for each of their soldiers that is still standing.

5. Once a soldier falls, remove it from the board.

6. Your teacher will read a description of each battle, which might change the rules a little bit.

7. The first side to win a total of four battles wins the American Revolution!

Materials Instruction Sheet

Soldiers

Each student playing a British soldier needs to make five soldiers. Each student playing a Patriot soldier needs to make three soldiers. Cut out the soldiers from the *British or Patriot Template Sheet* (pages 47–48) and put them together so they stand up. If you have time, color your soldiers.

Game Board

Copy the game board pictured below onto 11" x 17" poster board or construction paper. Once you have copied this game board, tape it down on a flat surface, such as a desk or the floor.

Patriots   British

B			E		B
A		C	D	F	A
B			E		B

Weapon Ramp

Each group will need to create one weapon ramp. You will roll a marble or a crumpled sheet of paper down this ramp to try to knock over the opposing side's soldiers. Cut out and fold the ramp as shown on the *Weapon Ramp Template* (page 49).

British Soldier Template

Directions: Cut out the soldiers and bases to make five soldiers for each person on your team.

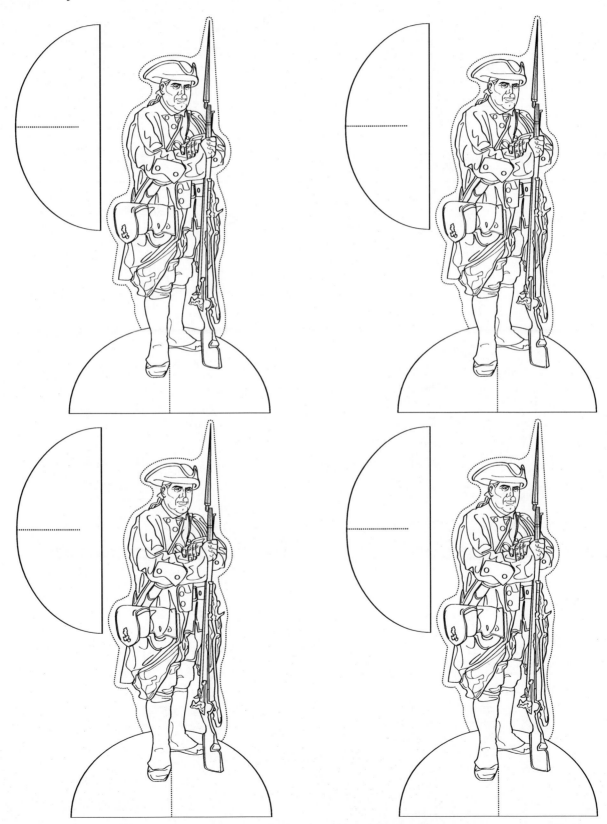

Patriot Soldier Template

Directions: Cut out the soldiers and bases to make three soldiers for each person on your team.

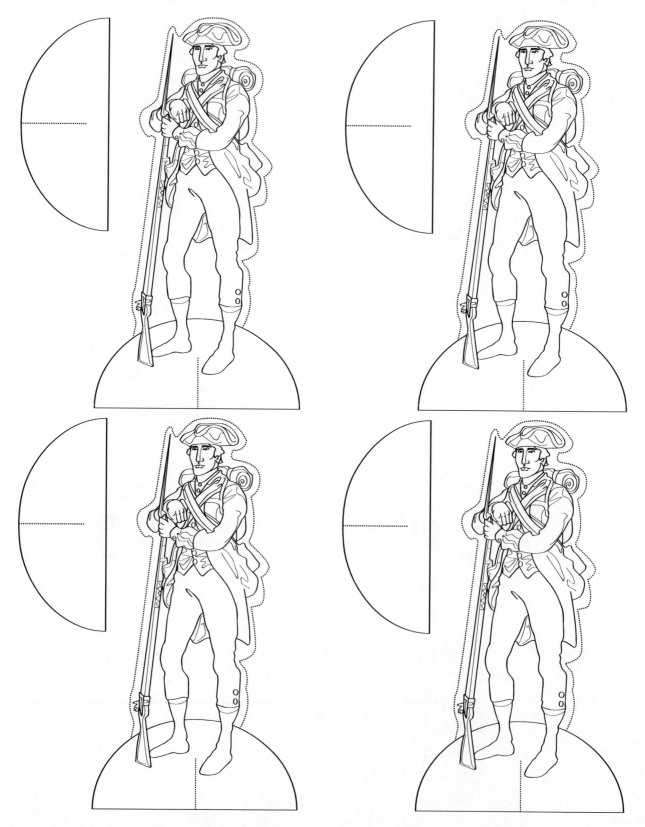

Weapon Ramp Template

Directions: Cut along the solid lines and fold along the dotted lines. Use tape or glue to hold the ramp together.

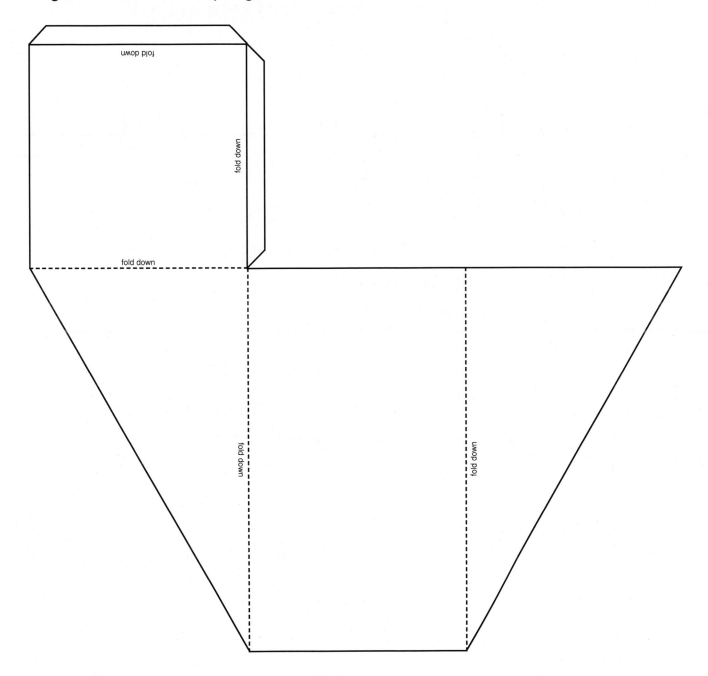

Habits of Mind Discussion

- What do you think was the most important factor that helped the Patriots win the American Revolution?

- Which was your favorite battle and why?

- Can you think of anything going on in the world now that reminds you of the American Revolution?

- In past American wars, has the United States ever been like Britain and our opponent ever been like the Patriots?

Jeffersonian Period

Overview

Students will role-play personalities of the Jeffersonian period and after previewing period issues using short reader's theater plays, will debate the issues in character. Character groups will vote on each issue with students earning dollars if they can successfully win others to their point of view. Following the debate, the student-characters with the most dollars will earn the right to run for president of the emerging nation, complete with campaigns and speeches. This activity previews issues and highlights the complexity of the Jeffersonian time period.

The total class time to complete the activity should be about four, 50-minute periods. You will measure student learning through discussion and evaluation of game activities.

Thomas Jefferson
Source: The Library of Congress

Objectives

- Students will examine the key ideals of the democratic republican form of government such as individual liberty, justice, and equality, and the rule of law. (NCSS)
- Students will appreciate the complexity of issues that faced the young nation and will learn about the ideas and personalities that influenced the outcome of these issues.

Materials

- copy reproducibles (pages 57–72) as described on page 52
- pencils
- lined paper
- poster board
- colored markers
- colored construction paper
- glue
- tape
- five 9" x 12" envelopes to hold group packets

Jeffersonian Period *(cont.)*

Preparation

Total preparation time should be about 30 minutes. Ask a parent to volunteer to help with the copying before you begin the activity.

1. Create hang-around-the-neck cardboard/paper nametags for use during the reader's theater plays. You will need: Thomas Jefferson, Alexander Hamilton, John Marshall, Abigail Adams, and Red Jacket.

2. Copy and post the appropriate day's *Student Directions* (pages 57–58). Refer students to these directions rather than repeating yourself or answering innumerable questions.

3. Create a 9" x 12" envelope packet for each group of five students. Each packet needs to contain the following:
   - *Campaign Materials Menu* (page 59)
   - *Money* (pages 60–61)
   - *Character Card: Thomas Jefferson* (page 62)
   - *Character Card: Alexander Hamilton* (page 63)
   - *Character Card: John Marshall* (page 64)
   - *Character Card: Abigail Adams* (page 65)
   - *Character Card: Red Jacket* (page 66)
   - *Reader's Theater Scripts* (pages 67–71), only one per group

4. Make an overhead transparency of the *Habits of Mind Discussion* (page 72) to use at the conclusion of the activity.

Directions

Day 1

1. Read the *Read-Aloud Introduction* (page 54) to the students.

2. Place your students in groups of five. Pass out the envelope packets you created above.

3. Give students time to choose characters, read the *Character Cards*, and introduce the characters to their group.

4. Each group has a specific *Reader's Theater Script* to perform. Give the groups time to practice their scripts.

Day 2

1. Read the *Read-Aloud Directions for Day Two* (pages 54–55) to the students. And, post the *Student Directions: Day Two* (page 57).

2. Have each group perform their reader's theater in front of the class and allow each group to discuss the issues and vote. Make sure students keep track of their groups' winning opinions and also remember their characters' amounts of money.

Jeffersonian Period *(cont.)*

Directions *(cont.)*

Day 3

1. Read the *Read-Aloud Directions for Day Three* (pages 55–56) to the students. And, post the *Student Directions: Day Three* (page 58).

2. Gather the materials listed in the *Materials* section of the lesson plan for students to purchase with the money they earned the previous day.

3. Using only the winning candidate's money, the group will purchase supplies from the *Campaign Materials Menu* (page 59), which they will use to make campaign posters and to write speeches. Remind students that speeches will need to include each of the winning character opinions from the previous part of the game.

Day 4

1. Read-aloud the *Read-Aloud Directions for Day Four* (page 56) to students.

2. The five candidates will display their posters and will give their prepared speeches in front of the class. Keep in mind that these new candidates are composites of all the winning opinions from each group. So, they will have made-up names and their opinions/political platforms will vary from group to group.

3. The class now votes their personal beliefs in choosing an overall presidential winner. If you like, hold another election with students voting among the real candidates (Jefferson, Hamilton, etc.).

4. Read the *Closure Read-Aloud* (page 56) to the students and close with the *Habits of Mind Discussion* (page 72).

Things to Consider

1. Jefferson and Hamilton have significantly more lines in the reader's theater plays than do other characters. You may want to put your more confident readers in these roles.

2. Included are parts for exactly 25 students (five groups of five). You may need to place more than one student on a part, ask one student to play multiple parts, or, with a smaller class, decide to skip one of the five issues (any will work).

3. While this game is a bit complex, it is broken into distinct "chunks," each of which should be manageable for your class. If your class needs extra help, you could include a copy of the day's quick directions with each group packet.

4. While arguing and voting on the issues may take up to 30 minutes, strive to reduce the time spent on issues (as students become more comfortable with the procedure).

5. If you would rather not hassle with copying and distributing paper "money," you can have students keep track of their winnings on paper.

Jeffersonian Period (cont.)

Read-Aloud Introduction

When the United States was a young country, there were many issues that needed to be worked out. Are we governed by law or by a president? Who has power in the government? Should we trust uneducated people to make important decisions with their votes? Should we put up with abuses from larger, more established countries?

Just like today, leaders had different ideas of what to do. Each of these leaders wanted what was best for the country and all were smart, but still they disagreed. It wasn't always clear exactly what was right and what was wrong. Sometimes a decision was good for some people in the country and bad for others. Other times, leaders had to compromise.

For the next few days, we will be playing a game in which each person will become a character from the early 1800s and will try to get people to believe in their ideas. We will use short plays to look at five issues and you will then debate the issues in your group. The character that gets the most people to believe in his or her ideas, wins.

We will be splitting into groups of five. In each group there will be a Thomas Jefferson, Abigail Adams, John Marshall, Alexander Hamilton, and a Red Jacket. Each character will get a sheet that explains who they are and also tells exactly what they believe about five important issues. The first thing you need to do is to explore your character and introduce yourself to the group.

Each group is also responsible for a short play that shows an important issue of the time. After you have introduced your characters, practice your play. You will be reading it aloud in front of the class tomorrow

Read-Aloud Directions for Day Two

1. We will begin today by having each group go in front of the class to present its assigned play.

2. After each play, discuss the issue in your group. Your job is to make the other people in your group believe what your character believes. No matter what you personally believe, try to make people agree with and vote for your character!

3. After you have discussed the issue, you will hold a vote. To vote, write down the name of the character with which they most agree. You cannot vote for yourself. So, you have to choose another member of your group.

Jeffersonian Period *(cont.)*

Read-Aloud Directions for Day Two *(cont.)*

4. The character that wins the vote gets $100. Each character that votes for the winning character gets $25. So, your goal is to make people vote for your character's opinion, but you also want to vote for the idea that wins. Money is included in your group packet for you to pass out after each vote. If there is a tie, then nobody gets any money!

5. Remember who wins each vote by circling his or her opinion on his or her *Character Card*. This is important later!

6. At the end of the five plays, discussions, and votes, the character with the most money, wins. Write how much money he or she has on his or her *Character Card*. This is important later!

Read-Aloud Directions for Day Three

The character in your group who earned the most money yesterday is now a candidate for president of the United States. However, what you will do is actually combine all the winning opinions from your group's votes yesterday. So, although the winning character gets to be the candidate, he or she must be recreated. You will work together to come up with a new name for the candidate. You will also have to define the candidate's views on all the issues.

The rest of the people in the group are the campaign staff. You will want a speech writer, a finance manager, a campaign manager, and a campaign artist. You may use only your candidate's money to buy supplies. You will use those supplies to create a campaign poster and to write a speech. You may use only the supplies that you buy. That means no pencils, pens, or paper unless you pay for them. You will only be able to buy supplies once and will need to show me a list of how you will spend your money before you can buy anything. Once you buy your supplies, clear your tables of everything except what you bought. Don't accidentally use anything else, or I might take away some of your money or supplies!

In your speech, you will need to use every winning opinion from the earlier debates (even if it wasn't your candidate's opinion). Remember, you circled each winning opinion on the character sheets. You will also want to make your speech sound good, as your candidate will be reading it in front of the class. Take your time to organize and write a good speech!

Jeffersonian Period *(cont.)*

Read-Aloud Directions for Day Three *(cont.)*

Work as a group to decide who is in charge of which task and how to use your time. Remember, the first thing you need to do is write a list of how you will spend your candidate's money. Then write a speech and make your campaign poster.

Read-Aloud Directions for Day Four

Your candidate is now on his or her own. You are no longer campaign staff and can vote for whomever you think is right. Each candidate will display his or her poster and give his or her speech. Then, the class will vote to determine the winner of the presidency of the United States.

Closure Read-Aloud

We know who won our classroom election, but who actually won the election of 1800? It was really close! It came down to a tie between Thomas Jefferson and a man named Aaron Burr, who was a Federalist like Alexander Hamilton. Burr was just about the meanest Federalist you ever met. He drank, he smoked, and he tried to push other people around.

But Alexander Hamilton hadn't voted yet.

Even though Burr was a Federalist, Hamilton chose Thomas Jefferson to be president of the United States! Jefferson and Hamilton might not have agreed in politics, but when it came down to a choice between disagreeing and disrespecting, Hamilton chose to go with the person he thought would be the best president.

Now, Burr wasn't too pleased with this. He wanted to be president and blamed Hamilton for his loss. So, Burr challenged Hamilton to a duel, and Hamilton accepted. Like the gentleman he was, Hamilton fired his pistol into the air, but when it was Burr's turn to shoot, he fired right at Hamilton, hitting him in the stomach and killing him.

After this, Jefferson went on to become a very important president and Burr fled to the West where nobody would put him on trial for the murder of Hamilton.

Student Directions: Day Two

1. Yesterday, you read about your characters and introduced your characters to the group. Then, you practiced your plays.

2. Today, after each play is shared, you will debate the issue, trying to make people vote for your character's opinion. These opinions are included on your *Character Cards*.

3. Vote by writing down the name of the character with whom you agree. Keep in mind that you can't vote for yourself. Count your votes to see who wins.

4. The character who wins the vote gets $100. Each character who voted for the winner gets $25. If there's a tie, nobody gets paid. Be sure that you keep track of your money!

5. Circle each winning character's opinion on the correct *Character Card*.

6. After all the plays, discussions, and votes, the character with the most money wins! Write down the winner's total money.

Student Directions: Day Three

The character in your group who earned the most money is now a presidential candidate. The rest of the group will help with the campaign.

1. Remember how much money your candidate earned yesterday. Write a list of what you want to buy with this money. Remember you can use ONLY what you buy!

2. Show your teacher the list and buy the supplies.

3. Use the following directions to make your campaign poster and write your speech sharing all the winning opinions from the day before.

   Poster: You need to now make up a new name for your candidate. Make a colorful poster describing your candidate and what he or she believes. These beliefs should be based on the winning opinions from your group the day before.

   Speech: Use every winning characters opinion from the debates to write your speech. It should sound good and should tell people what your candidate believes.

Campaign Materials Menu

Directions: Write a list of how you will use your money before buying campaign supplies. You may only buy supplies once.

Item	Cost
pencil	$50
lined paper	$50
poster board	$100
colored marker	$25
colored construction paper	$25
glue	$25
tape	$25

Money

Directions: Cut out the money along the dotted lines. Each group gets five $100 bills and twenty-five $25 bills.

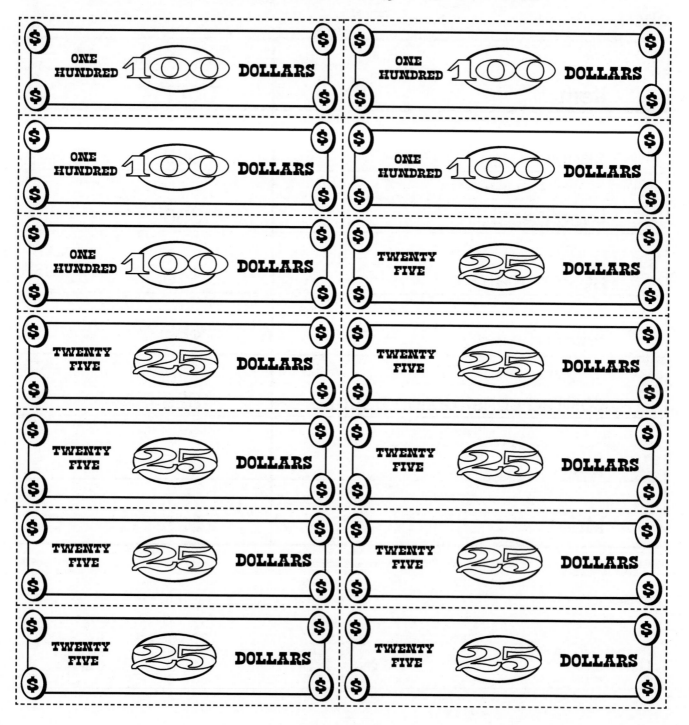

Money *(cont.)*

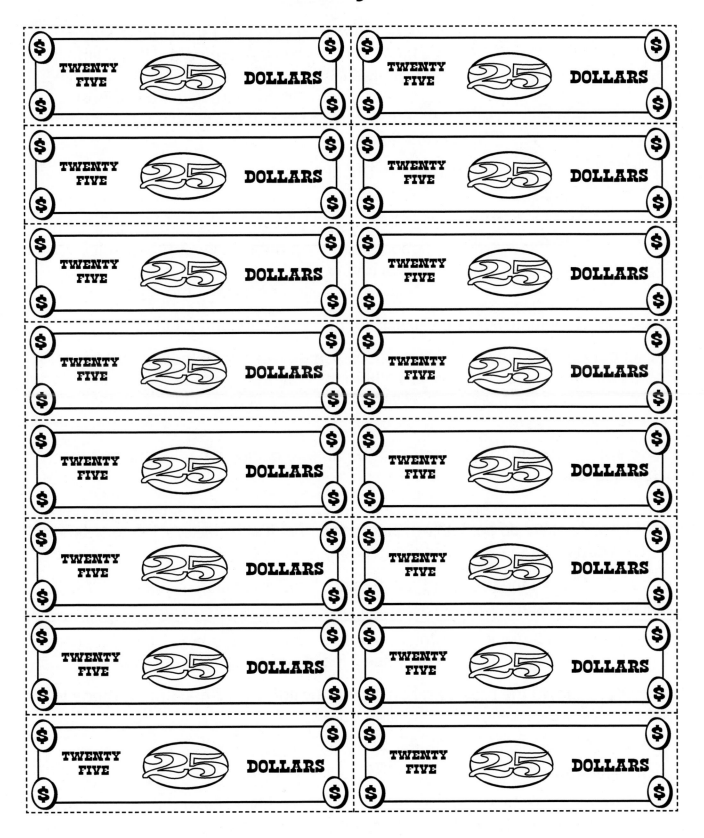

Character Card: Thomas Jefferson

You were the third president of the United States from 1801–1809. This was during a difficult time in United States history. You had to make many difficult decisions and sometimes there was no obvious right or wrong. Looking back, most people think you were a great leader.

Issue #1: Should every person have the right to vote?

> As a Democratic Republican, I think that people have the right to govern themselves, even if they choose to govern poorly. Every white man deserves the right to vote.

Issue #2: Should settlers be allowed to farm in American Indian territory?

> As our country grows, we need more space. American Indians will have to learn the ways of the white settlers, or they may choose to move to the other side of the Mississippi River, where there is certainly enough land for everybody.

Issue #3: Should the Supreme Court be able to decide what is and isn't constitutional?

> Each branch of government should decide for itself what is constitutional. If I accidentally do something unconstitutional it's the voters' job to tell me I'm wrong, not the Supreme Court's job.

Issue #4: Should the president act outside the Constitution to agree to the Louisiana Purchase?

> If we don't act quickly, we might not be able to get the land. I would agree to the Louisiana Purchase because I feel it is best for this country.

Issue #5: Should the president ban all trade with Great Britain and France to make those two countries stop stealing our ships?

> Yes. We will lose money in trade, but it's worth it to make a point and protect our people.

Real Quote—"Enlighten the people, generally, and tyranny and oppressions of body and mind will vanish like spirits at the dawn of day."

Character Card: Alexander Hamilton

After a strong military career and a friendship with George Washington, Hamilton was an author and great defender of the Constitution. He was also one of the leaders of the Federalist Party, who wanted a strong central government.

Issue #1: Should every person have the right to vote?

Who do you trust to make important decisions, an educated landowner or a lowly servant? I trust the educated landowner and think that he should lead the country with his vote.

Issue #2: Should settlers be allowed to farm in American Indian territory?

We have more important things to worry about than whether or not the Indians are happy. Of course settlers should be able to farm wherever they choose.

Issue #3: Should the Supreme Court be able to decide what is and isn't constitutional?

I don't care what happens with the Supreme Court as long as the Federalist judges appointed by President John Adams get the jobs they were promised.

Issue #4: Should the president act outside the Constitution to agree to the Louisiana Purchase?

In this new country, if we work outside the law, we risk showing that the law has no power and our president becomes a king. I would make a quick constitutional amendment that shows how the president should finance the Louisiana Purchase.

Issue #5: Should the president ban all trade with Great Britain and France to make those two countries stop stealing our ships?

No. Our trade is not important enough to Great Britain and France to make them change how they do things. In the end, all banning trade would do is hurt our merchants.

Real Quote—"Constitutions should consist only of general provisions; the reason is that they must necessarily be permanent, and that they cannot calculate for the possible change of things."

Character Card: John Marshall

You are the chief justice of the Supreme Court, appointed by President John Adams. You are a Federalist and believe in a strong central government. However, you don't think that one branch of the government should be able to make hasty decisions. You would like to see a balance of power among the judicial, legislative, and executive branches.

Issue #1: Should every person have the right to vote?

I believe that the job of government is to make hard decisions for people who aren't smart enough to make the decisions themselves. Because of this, I think that only smart people should be allowed to vote.

Issue #2: Should settlers be allowed to farm in American Indian territory?

As a Federalist, I am more concerned with promoting industry in our cities than I am about what happens with farmers and American Indians.

Issue #3: Should the Supreme Court be able to decide what is and isn't constitutional?

Congress and the president can do anything they want, as long as it's constitutional. It is the job of the Supreme Court to make sure they don't do anything that doesn't fit with this country's Constitution. Yes, the Supreme Court should have the power of judicial review.

Issue #4: Should the president act outside the Constitution to agree to the Louisiana Purchase?

The law is the law. If the law says I cannot agree to the Louisiana Purchase, then I would follow the law.

Issue #5: Should the president ban all trade with Great Britain and France to make those two countries stop stealing our ships?

As chief justice of the Supreme Court, I think we should make more laws to protect our ships and sailors.

Real Quote—"To listen well is as powerful a means of communication and influence as to talk well."

Character Card: Abigail Adams

You are the wife of President John Adams, who was in office just before Thomas Jefferson. While you agree with your husband's Federalist beliefs and support a strong central government, you are also perfectly capable of thinking for yourself. You are an early crusader for women's rights and especially the right of women to vote.

Issue #1: Should every person have the right to vote?

Of course every person should have the right to vote. Don't forget that women are people, too. Women deserve the right to vote, just as do all white men.

Issue #2: Should settlers be allowed to farm in American Indian territory?

If American Indian women can vote, then I think that we should adopt American Indian traditions, not the other way around.

Issue #3: Should the Supreme Court be able to decide what is and isn't constitutional?

The Supreme Court, like all courts, should be made up of my peers. Until there are women on the Supreme Court, I don't recognize its power.

Issue #4: Should the president act outside the Constitution to agree to the Louisiana Purchase?

The most important amendment we need to make to the Constitution is to give women the right to vote. Let's do that first and worry about the Louisiana Purchase later.

Issue #5: Should the president ban all trade with Great Britain and France to make those two countries stop stealing our ships?

We should ban all trade with Great Britain and France because they are repressive societies in which women cannot vote.

Real Quote—"If particular care and attention is not paid to the ladies, we are determined to foment a rebellion, and will not hold ourselves bound by any laws in which we have no voice or representation."

Character Card: Red Jacket

You are chief of the Seneca tribe and a great American Indian leader. Your name comes from fighting with the British in the Revolutionary War. However, since the war you have tried to make peace with the new American government. You are a fierce defender of American Indian ways and traditions and a strong promoter of the American Indian religions.

Issue #1: Should every person have the right to vote?

The native people have our own tribal laws and decisions are made by a group of elders.

Issue #2: Should settlers be allowed to farm in American Indian territory?

The Great Spirit has made this land for the use of all people and no one can own the land. The land deserves the respect and protection of people of all colors.

Issue #3: Should the Supreme Court be able to decide what is and isn't constitutional?

Will the Supreme Court enforce the treaties that white settlers choose to break? If so, the Supreme Court should have more power.

Issue #4: Should the president act outside the Constitution to agree to the Louisiana Purchase?

It's not your land to buy and sell. The Louisiana territory is already settled by many tribes.

Issue #5: Should the president ban all trade with Great Britain and France to make those two countries stop stealing our ships?

Learn from the American Indians the art of making compromises with stronger countries. I would ask Great Britain and France to stop stealing ships and then hope they hold to their word.

Real Quote—"Brothers, our seats were once large and yours were small. You have now become a great people, and we have scarcely a place left to spread our blankets. You have got our country but are not satisfied."

Reader's Theater Script—Issue #1

Should every person have the right to vote?

Teacher: It's 1800 and the characters stand in line outside a polling station. In the early days of the United States, any wrong decision could have resulted in the destruction of the country. The Federalists knew this and wanted only educated people making important decisions. The Democratic Republicans thought that every person should be able to vote, even if the person might not always be able to make the best choices.

Hamilton: The Democratic Republican's idea of everybody getting a vote sounds nice, but I would rather have only the country's smartest people making important decisions.

Jefferson: We just fought a revolution against Great Britain partly because they were taxing us without our consent! How can you say we should now make laws without part of our own population's consent? I think that every person should have the right to vote!

Hamilton: Common men don't have enough education to cast smart votes!

Marshall: I agree! If common men were educated, I say let them vote. But until then, it's just too dangerous to allow every man a vote.

Adams: I hear you debating whether or not all men should get to vote, but what about women? As I have said, "If particular care and attention is not paid to the ladies, we are determined to foment a rebellion, and will not hold ourselves bound by any laws in which we have no voice or representation." Mr. Jefferson, if you don't want to be controlled by a government without being able to vote for how it's run, why should women follow a government they can't vote for?

Red Jacket: Would you give American Indians a vote? The votes of the white man make laws over land to which you have no right. How can a vote affect the will of the Great Spirit?

Jefferson: As I see it, all people should have the right to vote, as long as they are white men.

Hamilton: Well, as I see it, our decisions are too important to trust to just anybody. I think only educated landowners should have the right to vote.

Reader's Theater Script—Issue #2

Should settlers be allowed to farm in American Indian territory?

Teacher: It's 1803 and characters sit in a circle, as if in an American Indian tribal meeting. Every year settlers move a little further west in search of new land to farm. Some people are in favor of forcefully removing American Indians from these lands. Others think the American Indians should learn to live like white people and become citizens of the United States. A very few people think we should respect treaties we had made with the American Indians and let the Indians keep their land.

Jefferson: I think American Indians should convert to Christianity, start farming instead of moving around so much, and learn to live like white people.

Red Jacket: As I have said, "You say there is but one way to worship and serve the Great Spirit. If there is but one religion, why do you white people differ so much about it?" You have your ways, and we have ours.

Jefferson: But, wouldn't it be easier to just adopt our ways and become citizens of the United States?

Red Jacket: No. You fought for freedom of religion; all we want is the same thing.

Jefferson: Then, you will have to move to the other side of the Mississippi River, where you will never be crowded by settlers.

Hamilton: Don't you think there's a chance we'll want that land, too, someday?

Marshall: Yeah, Jefferson, didn't you just send Lewis and Clark to map the land all the way to the other coast so that we could settle it?

Jefferson: Well, I can't imagine there could ever be enough people to crowd the great expanse of the West.

Red Jacket: As I have said, "Brothers, our seats were once large and yours were small. You have now become a great people, and we have scarcely a place left to spread our blankets."

Adams: Can American Indian women vote? Are they more respected than women in our society. If women are more respected, why don't we adopt your ways instead of forcing our ways on you?

Reader's Theater Script—Issue #3

Should the Supreme Court be able to decide what is and isn't constitutional?

Teacher: John Adams is a Federalist and at the very end of his term as president, he appointed 42 new judges, who also happened to be Federalists. Jefferson, the new president is a Democratic Republican. He doesn't like the new Federalist judges and has decided not to hire the 17 judges he likes least. One of the new judges-to-be, named William Marbury has asked the Supreme Court to tell Jefferson to give him the job he's been promised. There is a law called the Judiciary Review of 1789 that says judges have the power to tell elected officials what to do. At this time the Supreme Court doesn't have much power, and they are worried that if they try to tell Jefferson what to do, he might just ignore the order.

Jefferson: If the Supreme Court tells me what to do, I'll ignore the order.

Marshall: Well, as chief justice of the Supreme Court, I don't want my order ignored because then it would be obvious that I have no power.

Hamilton: I don't care what the Supreme Court does as long as the Federalist judges get the jobs they deserve.

Marshall: Hmmmmm, what should I do? I can't tell the president what to do, but I can't just sit here doing nothing, either.

Red Jacket: I'll tell you what to do. Why don't you focus your attention on more important matters? These judges can just try to get their jobs under Jefferson's leadership. We have bigger problems

Adams: Mr. Jefferson, you need to listen to the Supreme Court. My husband, John Adams, was president and his appointments need to be honored.

Jefferson: Oh, that scoundrel John Adams. I'm still not going to do what the Supreme Court tells me.

Marshall: Hmmmmm, I can't just sit here doing nothing. Or can I?

Teacher: Here's what happened. John Marshall declared the Judiciary Act of 1789 "unconstitutional," meaning this law was actually against the law. This meant that judges didn't have the power to tell elected officials what to do, so the Supreme Court couldn't tell Jefferson to give the Federalist judges the jobs. This process is called judicial review.

Reader's Theater Script—Issue #4

Should the president act outside the Constitution to agree to the Louisiana Purchase?

Teacher: The president can't use the country's money for anything he or she wants. It's 1803, the French have offered to sell more than 800,000 square miles of land in the West to the president for fifteen-million dollars. That's less than ten cents an acre! The president's representatives have to make a quick decision. Do you sign a treaty with the French even though the Constitution says you can't, or do you risk ruining the deal by getting further approval?

Red Jacket: Deal!? What deal? Land can't be bought and sold, especially when the land has traditionally been my people's since before the first Europeans set foot on this continent. And didn't you say earlier that the land west of the Mississippi would always belong to my people?

Jefferson: If we don't act now, the French might take back the offer. As our country grows, we need this land. The practical benefits are more important than following the Constitution.

Marshall: This is a country run by laws. If our president doesn't follow the laws, he is no better than the king of England.

Hamilton: I think we should buy the land from the French, but let's make a constitutional amendment that makes it legal first.

Jefferson: If we wait long enough to make an amendment, we might miss the deal. We all agree the Louisiana Purchase is good for the country. We would double in size and gain free use of the entire Mississippi River. Why don't we just do it and worry about the Constitution later?

Adams: We can't just put off such an important issue. When you say we can "worry about the Constitution later," you're really saying that you know what's best and everyone else should just agree with you. That is a very dangerous belief in a democracy.

Teacher: What should the young country do? Should the president agree to the Louisiana Purchase outside the rules of the Constitution, or should the president try to work within the Constitution and risk ruining the deal? Everyone wants the Louisiana Purchase, but at what price to our system of government?

Reader's Theater Script—Issue #5

Should the president ban all trade with Great Britain and France to make those two countries stop stealing our ships?

Teacher: In the early 1800s, Great Britain and France were at war. They needed as many troops and ships as they could get. The two countries were so desperate for new ships that they even "impressed" into service ships that just happened to stop at British or French trading ports. These countries would steal American ships and even make the Americans fight in their armies.

Jefferson: If they're going to keep stealing our ships, then we're going to stop trading with them. Eventually, the two countries will lose enough money that they will have to promise to stop impressing our ships and men into military service.

Hamilton: What about our citizens who depend on trade for a living? If we stop trading with France and Great Britain, almost all the people of New England will lose their jobs!

Adams: I'm from New England and I can tell you that an embargo would greatly affect all people in that northern region.

Jefferson: We won't be without trade for long. The British and French need the money they make from trading with us.

Hamilton: No they don't! We are only a small nation. Taking away our trade from the British and French won't make any difference to them and they will keep impressing other nations' ships into military service.

Red Jacket: Your concern with jobs and trade in New England is important, but keep in mind that my people are still dying of smallpox and being pushed from our traditional lands. Shouldn't we be focusing our attention on these domestic matters?

Marshall: I think we should create the Embargo Act of 1807. With an embargo, we would stop all trade with Great Britain and France.

Jefferson: An embargo would make the French and British stop impressing our ships into military service.

Hamilton: An embargo would have no effect on the French and British, but would crush the trading industry here in New England.

Habits of Mind Discussion

- What do you think was the most important issue facing the young nation in the Jeffersonian Period?

- What do you personally believe about each issue and why?

- Do you think it was possible to be completely right or wrong? Why?

- What difficult decisions do you think today's leaders face?

- Do you think that today's leaders have to make compromises? About what?

Tecumseh and the American Indian Experience

Overview

Students will explore the tribal traditions, frictions, and changing ways that mark the arrival of settlers in American Indian territory.

Working in small groups, students will represent American Indian tribes, the settlers of Indiana, Tecumseh, and his brother Tenskatawa. Amid simulated daily life, the two brothers will attempt to convince the tribes to unite against the influx of settlers. Unfortunately for the American Indians, the game is rigged, ending with the Battle of Tippecanoe just as alliances start to form. Students will especially appreciate the historically true ending in which an earthquake prophesied by the brothers occurs just as they said it would. But, it's too late to unite the tribes.

The total class time to complete the activity should be about one to two, 50-minute periods. You will measure student learning through discussion and evaluation of game activities.

Tecumseh
Source: The Library of Congress

Objectives

- Students will learn to empathize with both settler and the American Indian points of view. (NCSS)
- Through examining one specific situation, students will gain an overview of the issues that affected American Indian/settler relations in the areas east of the Mississippi River.

Materials

- copies of reproducibles (pages 80–100) as described on page 74
- textbooks or other reference materials
- salt dough (recipe on page 19)
- 8 bars of soap
- 9" x 12" envelopes to hold group packets
- craft sticks
- glue
- construction paper
- markers or colored pencils
- string
- 12 large paper grocery bags
- tape
- 12 plastic bottle caps

Tecumseh and the American Indian Experience *(cont.)*

Preparation

Total preparation time should be about 30 minutes. Ask a parent to volunteer to help with the copying before you begin the activity.

1. Create a 9" x 12" envelope for each of the following groups:

   - **Shawnee Indians:** *Shawnee Indians Information Sheet* (page 80), *Tribal Meeting Directions* (page 88), *Tecumseh and Tenskatawa Information Sheet* (page 85), and *American Indian Tasks* (pages 89–90)

   - **Miami Indians:** *Miami Indians Information Sheet* (page 81), *Tribal Meeting Directions* (page 88), *Tecumseh and Tenskatawa Information Sheet* (page 85), and *American Indian Tasks* (pages 89–90)

   - **Delaware Indians:** *Delaware Indians Information Sheet* (page 82), *Tribal Meeting Directions* (page 88), *Tecumseh and Tenskatawa Information Sheet* (page 85), and *American Indian Tasks* (pages 89–90)

   - **Creek Indians:** *Creek Indians Information Sheet* (page 83), *Tribal Meeting Directions* (page 88), *Tecumseh and Tenskatawa Information Sheet* (page 85), and *American Indian Tasks* (pages 89–90)

   - **Settlers of Indiana:** *Settlers Information Sheet* (page 84), and *Settler Tasks* (pages 91–93)

   - **Tecumseh and Tenskatawa:** *Tecumseh and Tenskatawa Information Sheet* (page 85), *Tecumseh Information Sheet* (page 86), *Tenskatawa Information Sheet* (page 87), *Tribal Traditions* (pages 94–97), and the *American Indian Definitions Sheet* (page 98)

2. Make one copy of the *Settlers War Sheet* (page 99) to be given to the settlers of Indiana towards the end of the activity as described in the directions.

3. Use rope, string, or tape to mark off a section of your room as Indiana. It should only be about 10 x 10 feet. Divide Indiana into two parts: settlers and Prophetstown. The four Indian tribe groups will actually work outside the "Indiana" marked section. The Indiana settlers will work inside, as will Tenskatawa and his tribal recruits. At the beginning of the game, Prophetstown should be relatively small. As the game progresses, you will need to move the Indiana divider, making the settlers' portion smaller and Prophetstown's section larger.

4. Organize needed crafts materials as listed on page 73, making them easily accessible. You will either need to put crafts materials inside Indiana, or designate one settler who is allowed to leave Indiana to get supplies.

5. Make an overhead transparency of the *Habits of Mind Discussion* (page 100) to use at the conclusion of the activity.

Tecumseh and the American Indian Experience *(cont.)*

Directions

1. Read the *Introduction Read-Aloud* (pages 76–77) to the students.

2. Then, split students into the following groups.
   - 4 American Indian tribes
   - 1 group of Indiana settlers
   - 1 individual Tecumseh and 1 individual Tenskatawa

3. Pass out the correct envelope packet to each group as described on page 74. Allow students ample time to explore their packets before beginning the first 10-minute moon during which students will work on their tasks.

4. There will be four moons total. During each moon, Tecumseh will go to one tribe of his/her choice and try to convince them to join his rebellion. If the tribe chooses to join Tecumseh, they will send one of their members to live in Prophetstown with Tenskatawa and will need to promise to give up all European ways. As recruits move to Prophetstown, you will change the size of the area labeled Indiana, giving American Indians more space and the settlers less.

5. As the game progresses, all groups will try to complete their individual objectives as described in their packets. The settlers in Indiana should eventually feel pressured for space. Tell students that if anyone steps outside of Indiana, American Indians or settlers, they will need to sit out for 10 minutes before rejoining the game.

6. The American Indians in Prophetstown know that once they complete all four of the *Tribal Traditions* sheets and the *American Indians Definitions Sheet*, they will be able to rebel against the settlers. Just before this happens, give the settlers a copy the *Settlers War Sheet* (page 99). This sheet gives the settlers the right to attack Prophetstown at any time, which they hopefully will do just before the American Indians are ready. Once the settlers attack, the game is abruptly over. Tecumseh's American Indian coalition has been defeated before it had a chance to act.

7. Read the *Closure Read-Aloud* (page 78) to the students.

8. Have Tenskatawa and the tribal recruits who studied with Tenskatawa in Prophetstown teach the class using the *Tribal Traditions* sheets. This is an important part of the learning that takes part during the activity and as such, you might want to preview the sheets yourself so that you are able to prompt as needed.

9. Close with the *Habits of Mind Discussion* (page 100).

Tecumseh and the American Indian Experience *(cont.)*

Things to Consider

1. Tecumseh and Tenskatawa have complex roles that require significant reading skills. Either put confident students in these roles or preview the roles with your selected students before the actual activity day. Make sure they know their jobs. Tecumseh travels to one tribe per moon and tries to convince them to join the coalition. Tenskatawa stays in Prophetstown and teaches the people Tecumseh sends to him and completes *Tribal Traditions* sheets.

2. Timing in this game is crucial to the outcome. Make sure you give the settlers their war sheet just before the members of Prophetstown finish their final *Tribal Traditions* sheets. You want the settlers to attack just before the American Indians are ready to launch their rebellion.

3. Within groups, much of the work is self-directed. Do your best to excite students about their group tasks, and make sure that in each group there are students who will hold the others accountable.

4. Settlers might get a bit cranky as their space in Indiana shrinks. Good! Let them complain about the tight quarters, and if anyone steps outside the Indiana boundaries, have them sit out for 10 minutes before rejoining the game. This also means you will need to organize all the needed materials inside Indiana, or allow one student to leave Indiana for supplies.

5. If, despite the game's heavy hinting, settlers fail to attack before Tecumseh has united the tribes, you can use this experience as a strong discussion of what could have been.

Introduction Read-Aloud

It's 1809 in Indiana and while life certainly isn't easy on the frontier, at least it's generally peaceful. Settlers and American Indians live side-by-side and even trade together. For many of the American Indians, living next to the settlers is easier than living next to the other American Indian tribes, whom they have been fighting for centuries. Also, it helps that there's enough land for everybody. But times are changing.

Imagine walking into your living room one morning and finding strangers sitting on the couch watching TV. After a few days, you find yourself waiting in line for the bathroom and the new folks have eaten all the good leftovers in the refrigerator. You're fed up, so you decide to move in with the neighbors. How do you think your neighbors feel?

Tecumseh and the American Indian Experience *(cont.)*

Introduction Read-Aloud *(cont.)*

It is the same in Indiana. Every day new settlers arrive from the east and American Indians are starting to be pushed from their traditional lands. As they move, they bump up against neighboring tribes. Sometimes there is bloodshed.

Adding to that, there are two proud American Indian brothers who refuse to leave their land. In fact, these two brothers invite members of all the tribes to move to Indiana to a place called Prophetstown.

Why would tribes who hate each other want to live together? Further still, why would they want to put more people into a place that is already stressed for land? These two brothers, Tecumseh and Tenskatawa, say that the Great Spirit is on their side. They promise the Great Spirit will make trees shake and white houses crumble to the ground to signal the time for all American Indians to rise up and take back their lands.

As you can see, something's gotta give.

Today, we will be dividing into small groups and role-playing the situation in Indiana. Some of you will be American Indian tribes and some of you will be settlers. We will also have one Tecumseh and one Tenskatawa—the two American Indian brothers—who will try to spread their message.

Just as American Indians divided their calendar according to moons, the time from one full moon to the next, our game is organized by moons, each of which is 10 minutes long. I will tell you when each moon has passed. In each moon, you will have tasks that you need to complete and decisions that you need to make. If Tecumseh is with your group, you will spend that moon in a tribal meeting. There are directions in each packet that will tell you what to do during the tribal meeting.

All the directions you need are included in your group envelope and each group has different directions. However, everybody's goal is the same: you all want to secure enough land to survive and want to pass this land on to your children. Remember, just because you are American Indian, doesn't mean you get along with other American Indian tribes. Everybody wants this land, and you need to look out for the best interest of your group and your group alone. Some American Indian tribes may succeed and others may fail!

When we split into groups, your first job will be to elect a chief or mayor. After that, follow the directions in your group envelope and do your best to survive!

Tecumseh and the American Indian Experience *(cont.)*

Closure Read-Aloud

In this game, the settlers yelled, "Attack!" but in real life, it happened a bit differently. While Tecumseh was in the South trying to recruit the Creeks into the American Indian coalition, Governor William Henry Harrison sent troops into Indiana. Tecumseh told Tenskatawa not to attack while he was gone. However, with the new troops in the area, Tenskatawa disobeyed his brother and attacked anyway. Tenskatawa told the American Indians in Prophetstown that while they were outnumbered, the Great Spirit would be on their side, the settlers' bullets would just bounce off of them.

Unfortunately, for the Indians, the bullets did not just bounce off of them. The American Indians of Prophetstown attacked too soon and were routed. They fled and Governor Harrison and his troops burned Prophetstown to the ground. This is called the Battle of Tippecanoe.

After the battle, most tribes deserted Tecumseh and his brother. They had seen that the Tecumseh and Tenskatawa's promises were no good and they no longer believed they could beat Governor Harrison and the United States Army. This was the last major chance for the American Indians to unite as one nation.

In the War of 1812, Tecumseh fought for the British. At the Battle of the Thames, he led an American Indian force onto the battlefield and the British deserted him, leaving Tecumseh to fight the United States Army alone. Tecumseh was killed and his vision of a united American Indian nation died with him. Within 30 years, almost all of the American Indian tribes in Indiana had been forced to move further west. Many American Indians died along the way, and more were killed in conflicts with the Plains Indians such as the Comanche. It could have been so different, if only Tenskatawa hadn't attacked too soon.

As a side note, remember when Tecumseh promised that the Great Spirit would shake the trees and crumble houses to the ground as a signal for all American Indians to start their fight? On December 16, 1811, the very day Tecumseh had prophesied, the New Madrid earthquake shook the United States. With a magnitude of over 8.0, the New Madrid quake was one of the most powerful in United States history. Great tracts of land were split apart and people felt the shock from New York to Alabama. Is this just a chance occurrence, or was the Great Spirit showing its alliance with the American Indians? The Battle of Tippecanoe was only a month earlier, on November 7. What would the world be like now if the American Indians in Prophetstown had waited just another month for the sign from the Great Spirit?

Tecumseh and the American Indian Experience *(cont.)*

Answers to American Indian Definitions Sheet (page 98)

1. **Moneto:** The Great Spirit or creator of the Shawnee people

2. **Pepoonki:** The grandfather of winter rules from the far north in Ice Mountain, but he runs away from the warm wind of spring.

3. **Melo'kami:** The grandfather of spring sits near the rising sun in the east and listens to all Shawnee prayers.

4. **Shawaki:** This grandmother is summer, warmth, and all things that grow. She brings the crops and pushes up the corn.

5. **Takwaaki:** After a long summer of work, the grandfather of autumn helps the Shawnee harvest their crops. He brings sleep and fullness.

6. **The three sisters:** maize, beans, and squash

7. **maize:** corn

8. **Bread Dance:** A ceremony held in spring and fall to celebrate either farming or hunting

9. **Tecumseh:** Shawnee chief who tried to unite the tribes

10. **Tenskatawa:** A medicine man, brother of Tecumseh, and spiritual leader of Prophetstown

11. **Prophetstown:** The town in Indiana where tribes gathered to learn from Tenskatawa and to fight settlers

12. **Shawnee:** American Indian tribe to which Tecumseh and Tenskatawa belonged

13. **Circle of life:** Shawnee belief that everything was connected: seasons, moons, compass directions, grandparents, crops, etc.

14. **The four grandparents:** Shawnee belief that a grandparent sits at each compass point and provides the Shawnees with the things they need. Grandparents also represent seasons.

Answer to Settler Tasks—Make Tools (page 93)

drawknife—used to take bark off trees

felling axe—straight-handled axe used to cut down trees

hammer—made out of a hard wood because iron was precious on the frontier

winnow—like a large screen; put wheat in a winnow and shake; light chaff blows away and leaves only wheat seeds

quern—used to grind wheat seeds into flour

Shawnee Indians Information Sheet

Though you had been living in Ohio for generations, after the Battle of Fallen Timbers in 1794, you gave up most of this land to white settlers. With Tecumseh, your leader, you moved into Indiana Territory, but many wanted to fight for their traditional lands in Ohio.

By the time of this game, many of the Shawnee people are no longer willing to follow Tecumseh. He and his brother Tenskatawa want you to give up all your white ways, including iron farming tools and guns, which make your life much easier. Are you willing to give up ease of life in exchange for a weak chance at reclaiming your lands? Also, are you willing to work with the other tribes, many of whom are your traditional enemies?

When Tecumseh visits your tribe, you will have to decide during a tribal meeting whether or not you will follow him. Until then, you are more worried about daily life. Complete the tasks below to the best of your ability. You will find directions on the *American Indian Tasks* sheets.

- make clay pots

- knap flint for arrowheads and knives

- make deerskin clothing

- play kokolësh

Miami Indians Information Sheet

You were once the most powerful American Indian tribe in the Ohio area. Under Chief Little Turtle, you defeated the United States Army in two large battles in 1790 and 1791. You were finally forced to leave the Ohio territory after the Battle of Fallen Timbers, in which you fought as allies with the Shawnee. While you worked with the Shawnee before, you are now competing for land in Indiana.

When Tecumseh visits your tribe, you will have to decide during a tribal meeting whether or not you will work with the Shawnee again. Until then, you are more worried about daily life. Complete the tasks below to the best of your ability. You will find directions on the *American Indian Tasks* sheets.

- make clay pots

- knap flint for arrowheads and knives

- make deerskin clothing

- play kokolësh

Delaware Indians Information Sheet

You were pushed out of your native lands in New Jersey and forced west, where you bumped into the Iroquois, who pushed you into Ohio. Once in Ohio, you gained enough strength to resist the Iroquois. Though you are one of the oldest American Indian tribes, called grandfathers by others, you have adopted many European ways including Christianity. You are heavily dependent on trade with white settlers and would certainly side with the settlers in a conflict with your traditional enemies, the Iroquois.

When Tecumseh visits your tribe, you will have to decide during a tribal meeting if you are willing to give up the white religion and your European ways for a chance at reclaiming lost lands in Ohio. Until then, you are more worried about daily life. Complete the tasks below to the best of your ability. You will find directions on the *American Indian Tasks* sheets.

- make clay pots

- knap flint for arrowheads and knives

- make deerskin clothing

- play kokolësh

Creek Indians Information Sheet

You live in what today is Alabama and Georgia. While you are called Creek Indians, you are actually a group of many tribes including the Choctaws and Chickasaws. You live far to the south of Tecumseh and the Indiana territory, but he and his brother still want you to join their alliance. Are you willing to fight the powerful United States Army when you still have enough land to live comfortably?

When Tecumseh visits your tribe, you will have to decide during a tribal meeting whether you will give up all your European ways and send a tribe member to live in Prophetstown. Until then, you are more worried about daily life. Complete the tasks below to the best of your ability. You will find directions on the *American Indian Tasks* sheets.

- make clay pots

- knap flint for arrowheads and knives

- make deerskin clothing

- play kokolësh

Settlers Information Sheet

1. You are the settlers of Indiana. From now on, you will need to stay inside the boundaries of the space marked Indiana. Go there now. If any members of your group step outside the boundaries of Indiana, they are lost in the wilderness and die. They will need to sit out for 10 minutes before they can rejoin the game.

2. Your next job is to elect a student to play Governor William Henry Harrison. Governor Harrison will be in charge of reading the rest of this sheet aloud and for making educated decisions. Elect Governor Harrison now.

3. Your goal is to farm the land and create a settlement. You will need to create laws and eventually build a church using the natural resources contained inside your portion of Indiana. Don't worry about what the American Indian tribes are doing. You will get more information later about how to deal with them.

4. You will need to choose how to use your time in order to create a pioneer society. Try to complete the following tasks:

   - build a church

   - write laws

   - farm the land

   - make tools

Tecumseh and Tenskatawa Information Sheet

Through Tenskatawa's vision and friendship with the Great Spirit, you know something that the other tribes don't know. The settlers will keep coming, and eventually they will take land from all the tribes. If the tribes don't work together **right now** and make a stand, no tribe will survive.

Your plan is to unite the tribes into one great nation, a nation strong enough to stand up to the settlers.

As brothers, you work together. Tecumseh's job is to travel to each tribe and convince them to send one tribe member to Prophetstown, Indiana. Tenskatawa is a spiritual leader, like a medicine man. His job is to stay in Prophetstown and teach the people who join him.

In the time of four moons, Tecumseh will try to unite the tribes. If he is successful and once four moons have passed all American Indians will rise up and try to kick the settlers out of Indiana.

Your individual information sheets will tell you exactly how to accomplish this task.

Tecumseh Information Sheet

Each moon you will visit **one** tribe and in the tribal meeting, you will try to convince them to do the following things:

1. Send one tribe member to live with Tenskatawa in Prophetstown, where they will learn American Indian traditions.

2. Promise that after four moons have passed, the tribe will unite with Prophetstown to fight the United States Army. The Great Spirit will make the trees shake and will crumble white houses to the ground to signal the right time to attack.

The tribes might not want to work with other tribes. And, they also may not want to lose one of their members, so you will have to be convincing. In the tribal meeting, use the following information:

- If we don't unite all the tribes **right now**, there will soon be too many settlers and we will all lose our land. This may be our last chance.

- Not only are we losing our land, we are also losing our culture and our tradition. Look around! We are all wearing the clothing of the settlers and we are even starting to believe in the settlers' God.

- The Great Spirit has told us all to stop using the settlers' ways. No more guns, no more alcohol, no more settlers' clothing, and no more Christianity. The Great Spirit will make the trees shake and will crumble white houses to the ground to show that the Great Spirit is on the side of the American Indians.

- "A single strand of hair is easy to break. But if we take all of our hair and braid it, that braid would be almost impossible to break. The different tribes must form that braid."

At the end of each tribal meeting, the tribe will vote on what to do. If they decide to send one of their members to live in Prophetstown, you can take one group member to Tenskatawa.

Remember:

- Each moon you will visit **one** tribe, you choose the order.

- In the tribal meeting, convince them to unite with other tribes against the settlers.

Tenskatawa Information Sheet

You are a spiritual leader and medicine man. The Great Spirit has given you a vision in which he told you to return to American Indian traditions and to stop living like the white settlers. Your job is to live in Prophetstown and to teach American Indian traditions to members of all tribes.

You live in Prophetstown inside the space marked Indiana. You and your followers cannot step outside this space. If anyone steps outside the boundaries in Indiana, they are lost in the wilderness and die. They will need to sit out for 10 minutes before they can rejoin the game.

Your brother Tecumseh will be traveling to tribes and hopefully sending tribe members to live with you. Here is what you need to do:

1. Complete the *Tribal Traditions One* sheet. Remember this information! You will need it to help teach the people who come to live with you.

2. When tribe members come to live with you, work together to complete the other *Tribal Traditions* sheets. You need to do the first sheet yourself, wait until you have two people (including yourself) to work on the second sheet, wait for three people before working on the third sheet, and four people before working on the fourth sheet.

3. If you have extra time or if Tecumseh does not send you enough people to complete the next *Tribal Traditions* sheet, you can work on the *American Indian Definitions Sheet*. If you finish this sheet, you don't have to wait for the right number of people in order to work on and complete the rest of the *Tribal Traditions* sheets.

4. Once you have completed all four *Tribal Traditions* sheets and the *American Indian Definitions Sheet*, the Great Spirit will send an earthquake signaling the time for all American Indians to rise up and take back the lands that rightfully belong to your people!

Remember that your goal is to complete the *Tribal Traditions* sheets so that you can kick the settlers out of Indiana. Once you complete the *American Indian Definitions Sheet*, you can complete the *Tribal Traditions* sheets without waiting for enough Indians. Also, stay inside the boundaries of Indiana!

Tribal Meeting Directions

When Tecumseh visits your group, you will have a tribal meeting that will last the entire moon instead of working on your *American Indian Tasks*. At the end of the meeting, the tribe will vote on whether or not to join with Tecumseh. If you choose to join, one of your members will need to accompany Tecumseh back to Indiana, where he or she will live in Prophetstown with Tenskatawa.

Here is how the Tribal Meeting works:

1. Tecumseh will have time to tell the tribe why they should join him and his brother. While Tecumseh speaks, the tribe should be quiet.

2. Your chief will have time to tell Tecumseh why it is difficult for the tribe to join him. While the chief speaks, everyone else needs to be quiet.

3. All tribe members may then discuss the issue with Tecumseh and among themselves. Listen to everybody's opinions.

4. When your teacher directs you, you will vote. Tecumseh may **not** vote.

5. If there is a tie, then Tecumseh may vote.

Remember that if you choose to join Tecumseh, you will be making an alliance with all the other tribes and you will have one less member to help with your tribal jobs.

American Indian Tasks

Make Clay Pots

Materials: salt dough or clay; construction paper; markers

Directions: Use salt dough or clay to make pots for storing dry goods and for cooking. In New Jersey, archaeologists found an American Indian pot large enough to cook two deer! Make at least three pots, mount them on construction paper, and write on the paper what each pot might have been used for (e.g., storing grain or cooking).

Knap Flint for Arrowheads and Knives

Flint is a hard stone that will hold a very sharp edge. Knapping was how American Indians chipped flint to make usable tools.

Materials: 2 bars of soap; 7 craft sticks; construction paper; pens

Directions: Carve soap to make at least five arrowheads and then attach them to craft sticks (arrow shafts) to make arrows. Also make at least two "knife blades" in the same way—attach your knife blades to craft-stick handles. Mount your arrows and knives on construction paper and then write a short description on the paper including the term "flint knapping." Use your materials wisely so that you have enough to complete everything!

Play Kokolësh

Materials: string, tape, craft sticks, plastic bottle tops

Directions: Tie about six inches of string onto the end of a craft stick (tape it in place if you need to), and tie or tape the other end of the string to the top of a bottle cap. Now, hold the craft stick and try to swing the bottle cap up and catch it on the end of your craft stick. Once one person in your group can catch the cap three times in a row, you have finished this task!

American Indian Tasks (cont.)

Make Deerskin Clothing

Materials: three large paper bags, scissors, markers

Directions: Much American Indian clothing was made from deerskins. You will need to make three shirts in order to finish this task.

1. Crumple up a paper bag, but be careful not to rip it.
2. Carefully straighten the bag.
3. Cut a hole in the top of your bag for your head and in the sides of the bag for your two arms.
4. Use markers to decorate your deerskin shirt.

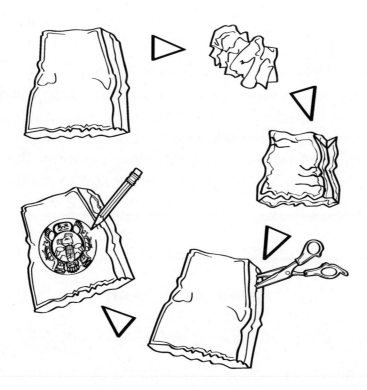

Settler Tasks

Build a Church

Directions: Use craft sticks and glue on a paper base to build a church. Your church needs to be at least two stick lengths long, one stick length wide, and four inches tall. It needs to have a sloped roof, a door, and a steeple (the part that sticks up and usually is part of a bell tower). You might need to break craft sticks in half to create an opening for your door.

Write Laws

Directions: The frontier could be a lawless place. Write at least eight laws for your pioneer settlement. Don't forget to write what the punishment is for breaking these laws! You might want to include rules for horse theft, land ownership, and marriage. Be creative!

1.

2.

3.

4.

5.

6.

7.

8.

Settler Tasks *(cont.)*

Farm the Land

Directions: American Indian farming practices were much different than European methods. Read the descriptions below and then make a poster where half shows American Indian farming and the other half shows European farming. On another sheet of paper, list at least five differences between the two farming methods.

American Indian

Instead of clearing land for crops, American Indians just expanded existing clearings in the forest. After killing only the first layer of trees, they would burn the clearing underbrush and work the ashes into the soil to provide fertilizer for their crops. They also planted many crops together, instead of putting only one type of crop in a field. By planting the three sisters (corn, beans, and squash) together, the beans helped put needed nitrogen in the soil, the corn provided poles for the beans to climb, and the big squash leaves shaded the ground and kept weeds from growing. After 15 years, the nutrients in the soil were mostly used up, so American Indians let the field return to natural woodland. American Indians also relied on crops that grew wild such as chestnuts, acorns, hickory nuts, blueberries, strawberries, fruit trees, and edible roots.

European

Most settlers used farming techniques similar to what you would see today if you went for a drive in the country. They planted only one type of crop in a field, which is why you might see wheat fields, cornfields, or another type of crop for as far as your eye can see. Settlers had more advanced tools than the American Indians and used iron plows pulled by horses or oxen. Settlers planted in neat rows, and tried to keep their fields useful for as long as possible by using fertilizer in the soil.

Settler Tasks *(cont.)*

Make Tools

Directions: On the back of this page, describe how you think settlers used each of the tools shown below.

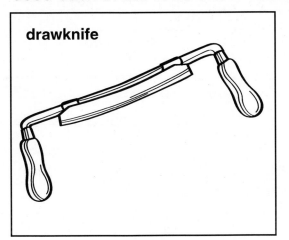

drawknife

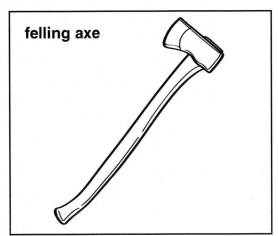

felling axe

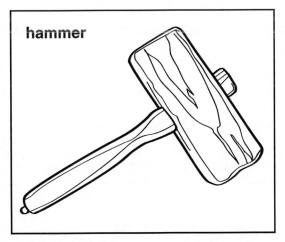

hammer

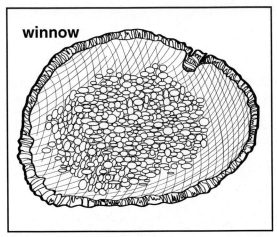

winnow

quern

Tribal Traditions One

The Shawnee Indians did not use the 12-month calendar that we use now. Instead, they kept track of the changing seasons by counting moons. Though the moons don't match up exactly with our months, they were pretty close. Here is how the Shawnee named their moons:

January	February	March	April	May	June
Severe Moon	Crow Moon	Sap Moon	Hal Moon	Strawberry Moon	Raspberry Moon
July	August	September	October	November	December
Blackberry Moon	Plum Moon	Papaw Moon	Wilted Moon	Long Moon	Eccentric Moon

1. How do you think the Shawnee came up with the names for their moons? Do the names have anything to do with the time of year?

   _____

   _____

   _____

   _____

2. Now, make up your own names for the moons of the year.

January	February	March	April	May	June
July	August	September	October	November	December

3. During the summer season, the Shawnee farmed the three sisters: maize (corn), beans, and squash. In winter, hunting and trapping were the most important jobs. The start of each season was marked by a sacred Bread Dance. The women ran the spring Bread Dance because they were in charge of farming. The men were in charge of the fall Bread Dance because they were in charge of hunting.

4. On the back of this page describe a festival celebrated in the United States that marks the fall harvest.

Tribal Traditions Two

Directions: Wait to start this sheet until you have a total of two people (yourself and a recruit living in Indiana) or until you have finished the *American Indian Definitions Sheet*.

The Shawnee called their Great Spirit Moneto. Unlike many religions, this God was seen as female. From her home in the heavens, Moneto wove a giant net. Eventually, Moneto would cast this net over Earth and the good would be pulled up to heaven, while the bad were left to suffer.

List three ways the Shawnee religion is like another religion you know:

1. _____

_____

2. _____

_____

3. _____

_____

Moneto had help from the Four Grandparents, one for each season:

Pepoonki: The grandfather of winter rules from the far north in Ice Mountain, but he runs away from the warm wind of spring.

Melo'kami: The grandfather of spring sits near the rising sun in the east and listens to all Shawnee prayers.

Shawaki: This grandmother is summer, warmth, and all things that grow. She brings the crops and pushes up the corn.

Takwaaki: After a long summer of work, the grandfather of autumn helps the Shawnee harvest their crops. He brings sleep and fullness.

On the back of this page, draw a colorful picture of each of the four grandparents. Use the whole page and do your best work. Under each picture, write a short description of each grandparent.

Tribal Traditions Three

Directions: Wait to start this sheet until you have a total of three people (yourself and two recruits living in Indiana) or until you have finished the *American Indian Definitions Sheet*.

Read the following Shawnee story, and then make it into a cartoon strip using construction paper and markers. Take your time and do your best work. At the end of this activity, you will be using your cartoon strip to tell this story to the class.

One day, 12 young men fell in love with 12 beautiful young maidens. But, these were no ordinary maidens. They were the daughters of Pepoonki, the grandfather of the north. The 12 maidens ran back to Ice Mountain where Pepoonki lived, and the 12 young men followed.

Now, it was not easy to travel in the northland. Eleven of the young men froze to death, but one was the grandson of Shawaki, the grandmother of the south. Just when he thought he could go no further, this young man asked his grandmother for help. Shawaki sent the warm south winds of summer to his aid, and Pepoonki, the grandfather of the north, fled from these winds. The young man was able to convince one of the maidens to be his wife and he brought her back with him to his village in the south. Sometimes even from the south, there blows a cold wind, and it is because one of Pepoonki's daughters lives there to this day.

Tribal Traditions Four

Directions: Wait to start this sheet until you have a total of four people (yourself and three recruits living in Indiana) or until you have finished the *American Indian Definitions Sheet*.

To the Shawnee, everything was part of the great web of life. The compass directions, moons, grandfathers, creator, and crops were all part of one cycle. Color the chart below. At the end of this game, you will use the chart to teach the rest of the class about the Shawnee Circle of Life.

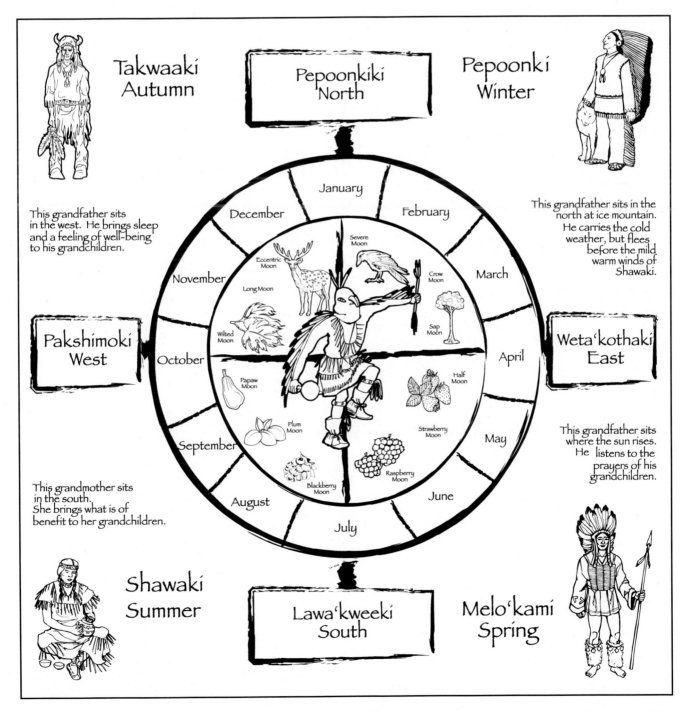

American Indian Definitions Sheet

Directions: Write definitions for each of the following terms. You can complete this sheet at any time. Once you are finished, you can start the *Tribal Traditions* sheets without waiting for the right number of people. Many of the definitions can be found on your *Tribal Traditions* sheets.

1. Moneto: _____

_____

2. Pepoonki: _____

_____

3. Melo'kami: _____

_____

4. Shawaki: _____

_____

5. Takwaaki: _____

_____

6. The three sisters: _____

_____

7. maize: _____

_____

8. Bread Dance: _____

_____

9. Tecumseh: _____

_____

10. Tenskatawa: _____

_____

11. Prophetstown: _____

_____

12. Shawnee: _____

_____

13. Circle of Life: _____

_____

14. The four grandparents: _____

_____

Settlers War Sheet

Read this quietly so that only your group hears!

Are you starting to feel a bit crowded? Maybe a little cramped? Are the American Indians using up all your natural resources? Well, pretty soon there will be more American Indians living next door. In fact, if Tecumseh and his brother Tenskatawa have their way, pretty soon Prophetstown will be more powerful than your settlement.

Or...

You could always attack them before they grow any stronger. In fact, you could attack them right now if you wanted. To attack the American Indians, you need to count to three and then all yell, "Attack!" as loud as you can. From now on, you can attack whenever you want.

Habits of Mind Discussion

- Was it fair for settlers to take American Indian land?

- Was it necessary for settlers to take these lands?

- What would have happened if Tecumseh and Tenskatawa had succeeded in keeping their lands in Indiana? Would it have made a difference to American Indians in the long run?

- Compare Shawnee religion to other familiar religions.

- Many American Indian stories, such as the one included on the *Tribal Traditions Three* sheet, explain why something is the way it is. Can you think of any other stories that are like this?

- In hindsight, should the American Indians have fought harder for their land?

The Civil War

Overview

Though small in scale, the battle of Fayetteville, Arkansas, demonstrates the larger realities of the Civil War, as the Union First Arkansas Cavalry meets the Confederate First Arkansas Cavalry in a place both call home. Students will role-play true inhabitants of Fayetteville, working as family and neighbors to create a historically true, three-dimensional model of the town. The class will then divide into North and South and will simulate the Battle of Fayetteville, demonstrating the horrors of brothers fighting brothers as well as many of the factors, such as rifled weapons and superior tactics, that eventually led to the Union victory over the Confederates. This activity is especially successful in inspiring excitement in boys who might otherwise have little interest in the Civil War. Thanks to historian Kim Allen Scott for help in creating a historically accurate simulation.

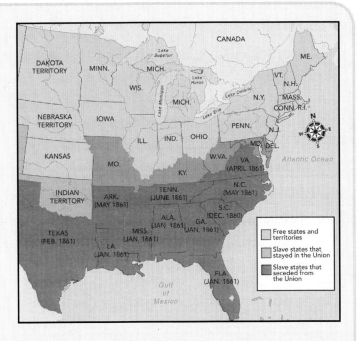

The total class time to complete the activity should be about two, 50-minute periods. You will measure student learning through discussion and evaluation of game activities.

Objectives

- Students will evaluate the role of physical geography in shaping human actions. (NCSS)
- Students will come to appreciate the idea of brother fighting brother as evidenced in the Civil War as a whole.

Materials

- copies of reproducibles (pages 111–128) as described on page 102
- glue or tape
- paint or markers
- one sheet of cardboard or plywood for map (as large as is convenient for your room)
- 28 index cards for stand-up characters

The Civil War *(cont.)*

Preparation

Total preparation time should be about 15 minutes. Ask a parent to volunteer to help with the copying before you begin the activity.

1. Copy and cut the *Fayetteville Characters* (page 111–124). You may want to assign students to the characters ahead of time.

2. Copy and post *Building Fayetteville* (page 125) and the *Fayetteville Map* (page 126). You may want a couple copies posted throughout the room.

3. Make 10 copies of the *Building Template* (page 127).

4. Organize a crafts area for painting or drawing the Fayetteville map.

5. Make an overhead transparency of the *Habits of Mind Discussion* (page 128) to use at the conclusion of the activity.

Directions

1. Read the *Introduction Read-Aloud* (page 103).

2. Distribute the *Fayetteville Characters* and spend the remainder of the first period creating your model of Fayetteville and the stand-up characters using the *Building Fayetteville*, *Fayetteville Map*, and *Building Template* sheets. To make your class numbers match the number of included characters (28), you may need to give more than one character to certain students, or put characterless students in charge of town building. With encouragement, students should be able to finish building the model by the end of the period, though time will be tight.

3. On the second activity day, or after completing the model of the town, read *The Battle of Fayetteville Read-Aloud Narrative* (pages 104–110). Have students move their characters and manipulate the model as directed. Depending on class size, you will want students to either huddle around the model, or place the model at the front of the class and have students approach the board only when they need to move their characters.

4. Finish with the *Habits of Mind Discussion* (page 128).

Things to Consider

1. The model of Fayetteville is large. If stacking copies for multiple classes have students use pens instead of paints and organize a bag of finished characters and buildings to be replaced on the board when needed.

2. Students may be disappointed when the models on which they worked so hard are destroyed. Use this valuable response to discuss how the townspeople of Fayetteville must have felt when their real homes and businesses were destroyed.

3. Not every character gets moved around much. Some students will place their characters once and then be finished. Allow students to add their own movements to make their parts more interesting.

The Civil War *(cont.)*

Introduction Read-Aloud

Nestled in the foothills of the Ozark Mountains, Fayetteville, Arkansas, is a beautiful little town. The old oak trees overhangs neat squares of well-planned streets and people take great care of their white fences.

At the intersection of Old Missouri and Cassville Roads, lives a retired professor named William Baxter. His trimmed hedge and smartly painted fence were the envy of the neighborhood. Even though Baxter no longer taught at the college, he liked living just north of the college grounds. He would stroll in the evenings and take in the mountain air, which he believed to have strong curative properties. Baxter was also a skilled doctor.

Across the street from Baxter lived Judge Jonas Tebbetts, who kept a Union flag hidden in his basement. Since the battle of Wilson's Creek in 1861, Confederate troops had lived in Fayetteville, but Judge Tebbetts hoped that the Union would soon win the Civil War. Most people thought the Confederate soldiers were a nuisance, with their supplies stored in Fayetteville schools, sick soldiers in private homes, and a newspaper office in the middle of the courtroom. People in town were related to soldiers on both sides of the battle.

A woman named Sarah Yeater, her son Charley, sister-in-law Sallie, and mother-in-law rented a house just across the street from Professor Baxter. Sarah was very proud of her husband who was away fighting in the Confederate army. She, too, hoped for an end to the war but wanted a different outcome than Judge Tebbetts.

Despite Fayetteville's college, hospital, and many nice homes, it was still a farming community at heart. Just south of Professor Baxter's house lived William McGarrah in his old farmhouse. He had founded the town in 1828 and had built the farmhouse with his own two hands. Most of the Fayetteville children were a little afraid of Mr. McGarrah. He owned large wheat fields north of town. In early fall, the golden wheat waving in the wind made a striking sight against the town's red oak leaves, just starting to change color. Can you imagine what it looked like at sunset?

These were not the only people who lived in Fayetteville. The Moores, Brannans, and Lees lived in a line of houses that stretched north from the main intersection. These three houses were very close to the Female Institute where young women trained to be nuns or could learn "painting in oil and water colors, pistil painting, drawing in pencil and crayon, pellis work, and all kinds of needle work." There were many other families who had houses southwest of the main intersection of Cassville and Old Missouri in the grid of streets that made up the majority of the town.

Today, we will be choosing characters and creating a model of Fayetteville. Because Fayetteville was between the North and the South in the Civil War, families and soldiers from both the Union and Confederate sides may help build our model. Use your character sheet to create a stand-up cardboard model of your character and then help to create the town itself. You will need to enlarge the Fayetteville map onto this base. Make sure you label each house and each location, and take your time to color them well. We will need to work quickly; we don't have much time to complete our model.

The Civil War

The Battle of Fayetteville Read-Aloud Narrative

Place the following characters or families on their homes: Baxter, Tebetts, Yeaters, McGarrah, Moores, Brannans, and Lees.

While it already wasn't easy living with Confederate soldiers in town, things were about to get much more difficult for the town of Fayetteville. In 1862, Union soldiers pushed south and the Confederate troops burned most of Fayetteville's business district before retreating. Why do you think the Confederate soldiers did this?

Destroy any buildings southwest of the Cassville Road–Old Missouri Road junction.

When the Union army marched into town, Judge Tebbetts hung the Union flag he'd been hiding in his basement from the front of his porch. How do you think he felt when the Union troops retreated from the town and the Confederates came back? It wasn't long before the Tebbetts family left Fayetteville. Sallie Yeater and her mother moved into the judge's old house.

Move Judge Tebbetts off the board. Move Sallie and Mother-in-Law Yeater into his house.

Meanwhile, the Confederate army was gone again, and a new commander was in town. Colonel Marshall LaRue Harrison and his Union army including the First Arkansas Infantry, the First Arkansas Cavalry, and the First Arkansas Light Artillery needed a place to stay. The regiment set up camp on the eastern slope of Mt. Nord. Colonel Harrison decided to move in with Sarah Yeater and her son Charley. He brings his son Edward to live with him.

Move Union Troops to Mt. Nord. Move Colonel and Edward Harrison into Sarah and Charley Yeater's house.

As you can imagine, it didn't take much of Colonel Harrison and his troops tracking mud into the living room and expecting meals at all hours of the day and night for Sarah and Charley to move in with the rest of the Yeaters in Judge Tebbetts' old house.

Move all Yeaters into old Tebbetts' house.

Unfortunately, Colonel Harrison wanted more space. So, he and Edward moved into the old Tebbetts house as well. This forces the Yeaters to live in a small shack in professor William Baxter's backyard.

Move Colonel and Edward Harrison into Tebbetts' house and move Yeaters to Baxter's shack.

William Baxter supported the Union army in any way he could, as long as it didn't involve physical labor. Professor Baxter saved the little hard labor he had left in his old bones for fixing up his hedge and keeping his fence in good repair and painted a sparkling white. When the Union asked the people of Fayetteville to help dig defensive trenches, Professor Baxter volunteered to help out in the hospital instead. He liked it so much, he worked at the hospital until Doctors Ira Russell and Seymour Carpenter arrived from St. Louis to take charge of the hospital. For Professor Baxter's good service at the hospital, he got assurance from the Union army that they would not disrupt his precious house and yard.

Place Dr. Carpenter in the hospital.

The Civil War *(cont.)*

The Battle of Fayetteville Read-Aloud Narrative *(cont.)*

One afternoon Professor Baxter looked out his window to see two Union soldiers taking apart his fence. This sort of thing happened a lot around town. Soldiers needed wood for barracks, blockades, and firewood, but the Union army had promised Professor Baxter that no harm would come to his yard. When Professor Baxter told one of the soldiers, Lieutenant Crittenden C. Wells, to stop tearing up his favorite fence, the lieutenant threatened Professor Baxter with a pistol.

Place Lieutenant Wells and Baxter in Baxter's yard.

The old professor explained the promise again. Lieutenant Wells gruffly let Baxter go on his way. Professor Baxter knew that sometimes ugly things happen in the middle of a war, but he decided that he no longer wanted any part of it. He and his family moved to Ohio where they didn't have to worry about soldiers in their front yard.

Remove Baxter from board. Return Lieutenant Wells to Mr. Nord.

No sooner did Professor Baxter leave, than the Davis family moved into the empty home. Joseph Davis was gone while he served in the Confederate army, but that doesn't mean that his wife, her sister, his slow-witted brother Ben, and their four daughters couldn't live in a Union town. It was such a nice house that Lieutenant Elizur Harrison, Colonel Harrison's brother, also took a room in the Baxter house.

Move Elizur Harrison, Mrs. Davis and family, and Ben Davis into the Baxter house.

While the Union army was settling into Fayetteville, the Confederate army under the leadership of Brigadier General William L. Cabell was massing in the town of Ozark, just to the south of Fayetteville. All told, Cabell had 900 soldiers, including the Confederate First Arkansas Cavalry, and two powerful cannons. Fayetteville was the southernmost outpost of the Union army and the Confederate General Cabell wanted to make sure the Union never got any further into southern territory. The Union army in Fayetteville knew there were Confederate troops in Ozark, and decided to keep a close eye on them. Colonel Harrison sent Lieutenant Joseph S. Robb down the road to Ozark to see what was up.

Move Lieutenant Robb to edge of board south of town.

But General Cabell and the Confederate troops were tricky. Instead of just coming straight up the road, they detoured to the west and turned north on the other side of the Boston Mountains. They moved north until they were almost right next to Fayetteville before hiking up and over the Boston Mountains.

Move the Confederate Troops and the First Arkansas Cavalry west, then north, until almost even with Fayetteville (but still just off the board).

When Lieutenant Robb returned to Fayetteville, he reported no Confederate activity in the direction of Ozark, and the Union army relaxed.

Move Lieutenant Robb back to Mt. Nord. Place Union Lookouts just south of McGarrah's farmhouse.

The Civil War *(cont.)*

The Battle of Fayetteville Read-Aloud Narrative *(cont.)*

Little did the Union army know that the Confederates had planned a surprise attack for dawn. Undetected, General Cabell and the Confederate army cut east and into the large sheltered ravine that led to Mt. Sequoyah and the high ground that overlooked Fayetteville. After quickly overwhelming a few lookouts, the Confederate army continued north on Mountain Road and got ready to attack.

Move Confederate Troops and the First Arkansas Cavalry north on Mountain Road until they are halfway to Old Missouri Road. Remove Union Lookouts from board.

It was a cold April morning, and Lieutenant Elizur Harrison had the covers pulled up to his nose. When he heard an unusual noise, he reluctantly got up, looked out his back door, and saw Confederate cavalry soldiers on horseback! He scrambled to get his clothes on and ran out the front door toward the Union regiment camp on Mt. Nord. Luckily, his brother, the colonel, was just ahead of him and they ran to the regiment to find the Union troops frantically getting ready under the shouted commands of the company officers.

Move Lieutenant, Colonel and Edward Harrison into the Union regiment camp on Mt. Nord.

It was a rough morning for the Yeaters as well. Sarah was sick in bed, and even sicker of living in the shack behind Professor Baxter's old house. Sarah heard the clinking and clanking of the Confederate army but said, "Let them come. I'm too sick to get up." Luckily Sarah had a smart mother-in-law, who forced her to get out of bed and, with the rest of the family, found shelter in the Baxter basement along with the Davis family and a few servants. What do you think it was like with all those people in one basement? Do you think it was scary to know a battle was coming, and be stuck in a dark basement?

Move all Yeaters into the Baxter house with the Davis family.

Meanwhile, the Confederate army was ready. General Cabell ordered soldiers on foot, called skirmishers, to rush into town from the ravine to try to take the arsenal buildings where the Union army kept their guns and ammunition.

Move Confederate Skirmishers west from Mt. Sequoyah to near the Cassville Road.

In charge of the Confederate artillery was Captain William Hughey, and as soon as the cannons were ready, he started firing at the Union regiment camp across town on Mt. Nord. The Union army, amidst whistling cannon balls and completely taken by surprise, looked like it might turn tail and run. And this is just what General Cabell counted on.

The Union army in Arkansas had a well-deserved reputation for running away when the battle got tough. General Cabell thought that with a surprise attack and an early show of force, the Union army would run for the hills like scared squirrels.

Place Captain Hughey on Mt. Sequoyah facing Mt. Nord.

The Civil War *(cont.)*

The Battle of Fayetteville Read-Aloud Narrative *(cont.)*

For a while it looked like this is just what was going to happen. About 30 soldiers stopped getting ready for battle, grabbed horses, and made a run for it. Among them was Lieutenant Crittenden Wells, the same officer who had threatened old professor Baxter. Apparently, Lieutenant Wells wasn't so brave when he was facing a real opponent.

Move Lieutenant Wells off the north end of the board, following the Cassville Road.

The next movement of the Union troops was also backward. At this point in the Civil War, both sides were pretty ragged. Some men were sick, some were recovering from injuries, and most were without uniforms. Some Union soldiers were barefoot and some had never even got their guns. Colonel Harrison ordered all the soldiers without uniform to the back side of Mt. Nord so that the uniformed Union soldiers wouldn't mistake them for the enemy and accidentally shoot them. Unfortunately, this was almost half of Colonel Harrison's army, leaving him with only 500 soldiers to try to hold the town against the 900 Confederate troops and their powerful cannons.

Move all Union Soldiers Without Uniforms off the board to the west of Mt. Nord.

It didn't look good for Colonel Harrison and the Union army. Amid raining cannon fire and Confederate skirmishers pushing up from the south, Captain Hopkins and Lieutenant Messinger told Colonel Harrison the battle was already lost. The best thing to do would be to retreat with whomever they could still save. But the Union army didn't have enough horses to retreat. They would have to fight.

Quickly, Colonel Harrison sent Major Ezra Fitch and the companies to the ruins of the Female Institute to try to hold the ground against the Confederate skirmishers and ensure the Confederates didn't get control of the Union guns and ammunition.

Move Major Fitch to the Female Institute.

Major Fitch got to the Female Institute just in time and took shelter behind the stone ruins of the institute's foundation. No sooner had Major Fitch ducked his head behind the foundation than Confederate troops rushed out of Tin Cup Ravine in an attempt to take the houses on the east side of the Cassville Road, including Judge Tebbetts' old house and the Baxter house, where the Yeater and the Davis families hid in the basement.

Move Confederate Skirmishers to just east of the Cassville Road.

The Confederates still expected the Union troops to retreat in fear, but as they closed in on the two houses, they were met by fierce resistance from Union troops stationed in the upper floors of the two houses. General Cabell couldn't believe it! The Union troops were actually fighting back instead of running away. He decided to take matters into his own hands. General Cabell dismounted and aimed one of the cannons, called howitzers, at the top floor of the Baxter house, where he could see the puffs of smoke from Union rifles. The cannon roared and apparently General Cabell remembered his West Point artillery training, because the ball went right in the upstairs window of the Baxter house.

Place General Cabell on Mt. Sequoyah.

The Civil War (cont.)

The Battle of Fayetteville Read-Aloud Narrative (cont.)

Unfortunately for Cabell, the cannon ball didn't explode in the upstairs room where the Union troops were still shooting, but went right through the floor. The cannon ball dropped from the upstairs, hit the kitchen floor, and kept going, landing right in the basement where the Yeater and the Davis families were huddled together. As dust and splinters sifted into the basement, everyone held their breath while they waited for the cannonball to explode. What else could they do? But in an amazingly lucky event, the cannonball had first hit a kitchen kettle, and the fuse had gone out. The families in the basement were safe, for now. The Union defenders couldn't hold off the Confederate charge and rebel soldiers burst through the kitchen door of the Baxter home.

Move Confederate Skirmishers into the Baxter house.

Soon the house was quiet. Ben Davis went upstairs and tried to tell the Confederate soldiers about the families in the basement so the soldiers would not burn the house. As Ben put his hand on a soldier's shoulder, another soldier shot him in the back.

Take Ben Davis's character off the board.

While the Confederates were forcing their way into houses on the east side of the Cassville Road, Colonel Harrison organized as many Union troops as he could find and advanced behind the Lee, Brannan, and Moore houses on the west side of the road. The families had to go into hiding.

Move Colonel and Edward Harrison and Union Troops toward main intersection, behind row of west-side houses. Move the Lees, Brannans, and Moores to McGarrah's wheat fields.

Who would think that a little spiral carved in the barrel of a gun could make any difference to the outcome of a battle? The Union army had rifled barrels, which made the bullets spin, and these spinning bullets could go about five times as far as the old duck hunting guns the Confederates carried. From behind the west-side houses Harrison and the Union troops could fire at the Confederate soldiers, but the Confederates couldn't fire back. Soon the Confederates were forced to retreat back to Tin Cup Ravine. This time, McGarrah was kicked out of his home.

Move Confederate Skirmishers out of the Baxter House and into Tin Cup Ravine. Move McGarrah to his wheat fields with the other families.

But the Confederates still had their cannons high up on Mt. Sequoyah. Captain Hughey and General Cabell continued to shoot cannon balls at the Union troops on the west side of the intersection, especially at Major Fitch and the others that ducked behind the ruins of the Female Institute. Why wouldn't these Union soldiers run away like they had before? With Union troops hiding behind the thick stone foundation of the Institute, Captain Hughey and General Cabell decided to stop firing the cannons, for now. Maybe if they moved further north along the mountain road, they would be able to shoot at Colonel Harrison and the others, who were just blocked by a small hump in the mountain.

The Civil War *(cont.)*

The Battle of Fayetteville Read-Aloud Narrative *(cont.)*

Fortunately for the Union, Colonel Harrison had already thought of this. He sent his brother and Lieutenant Robb (remember the guy who scouted the road south to Ozark?) to make sure the Confederates couldn't move into Mcgarrah's wheat field to the north.

Move Elizur Harrison and Lt. Robb into McGarrah's wheat fields.

Because of their rifled guns, Harrison, Robb, and the Union troops could shoot at the Confederates before the Confederates could shoot back. They kicked all the Confederates out of the wheat field and they took aim at the puffs of smoke that showed where the Confederate cannons were, high up on Mt. Sequoyah. With bullets whistling through the tree branches, Cabell and Captain Hughey retreated with their cannons back down the road to the south.

Move all Confederate soldiers still on Mt. Sequoyah down Mountain Road to south.

At the beginning of the morning, it looked like the Confederates would win the battle easily, but now the tables had turned and things were getting desperate for Cabell and the Confederate troops. He couldn't believe the Union soldiers were actually putting up a fight! Cabell knew that he just had to find the right way to scare the Union into retreat. General Cabell ordered all Confederate soldiers who had stayed behind to hold the horses to mount, about 275 people in all. Quietly, they moved into Tin Cup Ravine.

Move all Confederate Horse Holders into Tin Cup Ravine.

For a minute everything was still. Major Fitch reloaded and looked around from the ruins of the Female Institute. Elizur Harrison hurried back from the wheat field and hid near the Tebbetts house. Dr. Carpenter looked up from his work at the hospital and thought to himself that Fitch looked like a slow-witted turtle. Carpenter didn't much like Major Fitch.

Move Elizur Harrison from wheat field to Tebbetts house.

And Colonel Harrison got nervous. He knew something big was about to happen. "Aim low, boys," he told his troops, "and take good aim." After three hours of battling, most Union troops were desperately low on ammunition. Colonel Harrison didn't know if they had enough bullets to withstand a full assault. Suddenly, a bugle sounded from Tin Cup Ravine and the Union troops heard the snorting and stamping of many horses, and the jingling of harnesses and swords. The Union troops at the intersection gritted their teeth and clutched their weapons with white knuckles—some wanted to sneak away, but Colonel Harrison stood confidently with a cold glint in his eye.

Up the Cassville Road came all 275 Confederate soldiers! Hooves thundered and the soldiers yelled and waved their swords! Surely, thought General Cabell, the Union soldiers would turn and run from such a force.

Move all Confederate Horse Holders north on Cassville Road to the main intersection.

The Civil War *(cont.)*

The Battle of Fayetteville Read-Aloud Narrative *(cont.)*

But the Union soldiers held firm. They waited until the Confederate charge was only about 40 yards from the intersection before firing with their accurate, rifled guns. The streets had funneled the Confederate horsemen into a compact target for the Union defenders. As the first riders went down, the ones behind couldn't keep running. In disarray, the Confederate cavalry reared and looked for an escape from the deadly Union crossfire that seemed to come from all sides.

> *Turn all Confederate troops so they face south on Cassville Road.*

General Cabell couldn't believe it! Even in the face of stampeding horses, the Union troops had refused to retreat! The remaining horses and riders galloped down the Cassville Road before cutting through the grounds of the old college and back into Tin Cup Ravine.

> *Move all Confederate Horse Holders down the Cassville Road and then east into Tin Cup Ravine.*

The battle was over and General Cabell's gamble had failed! The remaining Confederate skirmishers retreated as best they could, and General Cabell assembled his remaining troops on the road leading south out of town. There weren't nearly as many as had started the day.

> *Move all Confederate troops to the road south of town.*

Dr. Carpenter rushed forward to tend to the wounded. Even the Confederate wounded were brought into the hospital. To Dr. Carpenter, every person who had fought that day was just a poor Arkansas boy who deserved his best treatment regardless of the side they had chosen. Elizur Harrison also helped the wounded Confederates, bringing water to the people who called out for it. The Yeater and Davis families emerged from the basement of the Baxter house, lucky to be alive. Within a year, Sallie Yeater, whose sister was married to a Confederate soldier, would marry Elizur Harrison.

Colonel Harrison stood amid the wreckage of the battle, feeling empty and proud. He would later write of the soldiers who had died:

> Green be their mossy graves
>
> Immortal be their name;
>
> Above, their banner proudly waves
>
> While heaven records their fame!

About a week later, Colonel Harrison responded to orders from his superiors and, along with the entire Union garrison, left Fayetteville. Eleven days later, the Confederates walked into Fayetteville, taking the town without a fight.

Fayetteville Characters

William Baxter

You are a retired preacher and former college professor. You believe in the Union, but your greatest wish is to live a nice quiet life, filled with walks on the campus grounds and puttering in the well-kept yard of your house, near Fayetteville's main intersection.

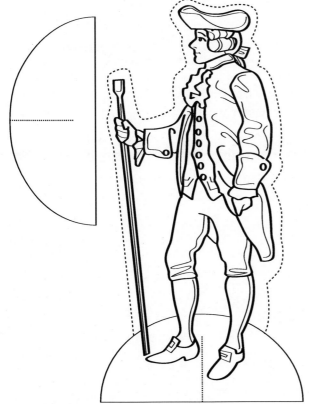

Judge Jonas Tebetts

When the Confederate army controlled Fayetteville, you kept a Union flag hidden in your basement. You are a fair-minded judge who won't be told what to think and you own one of the grand old houses near Fayetteville's main intersection.

Fayetteville Characters *(cont.)*

Sarah Yeater

You recently moved to Fayetteville with your son, Charley, your sister-in-law, Sallie, and your mother-in-law. Your family rents a house near the main intersection of town. You are married to a Confederate soldier, who is away fighting the Civil War.

Sallie Yeater

You recently moved to Fayetteville with your mother, your sister-in-law Sarah, and her son Charley. Your family rents a house near the main intersection of town.

Fayetteville Characters (cont.)

Mother-in-Law Yeater

You recently moved to town with your daughter Sallie, your daugher-in-law Sarah, and her son Charley. Your family rents a house near the main intersection of town.

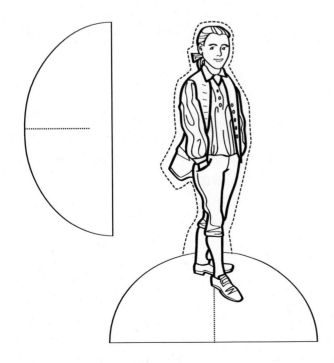

Charley Yeater

You are 11 years old and recently moved to town with your mother Sarah and two other family members. Your father is a Confederate soldier away fighting the Civil War. Your family rents a house near the main intersection of town.

Fayetteville Characters *(cont.)*

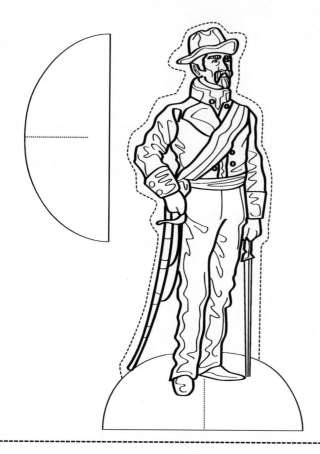

Colonel Marshall Harrison

You are the commander of all Union troops in Fayetteville. You are deeply embarrassed by the First Arkansas Calvary's cowardly retreat at previous battles.

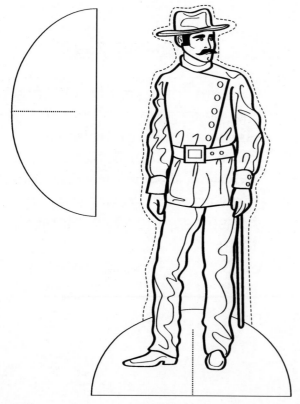

Lieutenant Elizur Harrison

You are the younger brother of Colonel Harrison, the commander of all Union troops in Fayetteville. As a young lieutenant, you hope to soon move up the ranks within the Union army.

Fayetteville Characters (cont.)

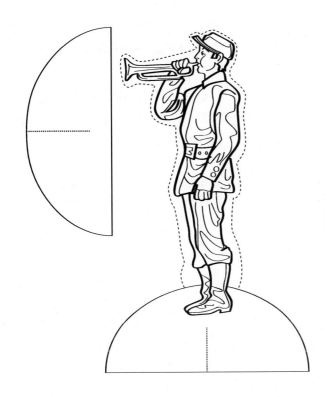

Edward Harrison

You are 12 year old and the son of Colonel Harrison, the commander of all Union troops in Fayetteville. You have recently been appointed bugler for cavalry company F, but spend most of your time with your father.

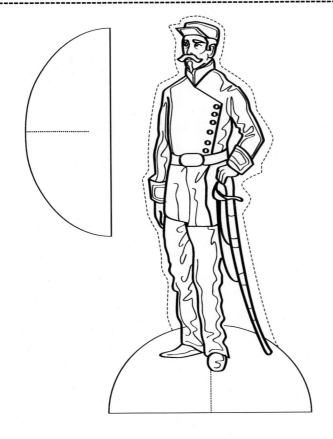

Lieutenant Crittenden C. Wells

You are a lieutenant in the Union army under the command of Colonel Harrison, but you think you deserve much better. You also think all the Fayetteville townsfolk are Confederates, and you boss them around every chance you get.

Fayetteville Characters *(cont.)*

Mrs. Davis and Family

You are the wife and family of a Confederate soldier who is away fighting the Civil War. In the family are Mrs. Davis, her sister, four daughters, and the husband's mentally-challenged brother Ben.

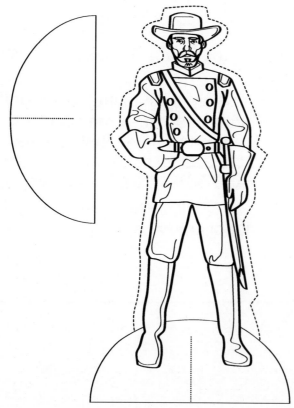

Brigadier General William Cabell

You are commander of all Confederate troops in the area. You are convinced that all Arkansas Union soldiers are cowards.

Fayetteville Characters *(cont.)*

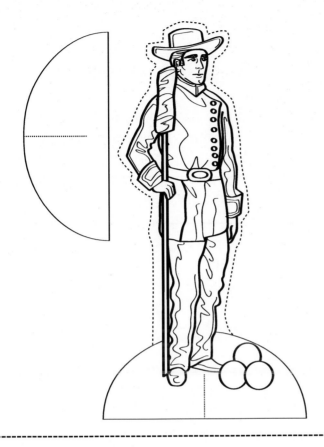

Captain William Hughey

You are in charge of the Confederate artillery (cannons), under the command of General Cabell.

Lieutenant Joseph S. Robb

You are a lieutenant in the Union First Arkansas Cavalry army under the command of Colonel Harrison. You are young and brave.

Fayetteville Characters *(cont.)*

Union Lookouts

You are members of the Union army under the command of Colonel Harrison and have dug holes called pickets south of town, where you keep a lookout for any Confederate activity in the area.

William McGarrah

You founded the town of Fayetteville in 1828, and are now an old, crotchety farmer who lives in an old farmhouse east of town. Your wheat fields extend far to the north.

Fayetteville Characters (cont.)

Moores

You are a good Fayetteville family, who own a nice house just north of the town's main intersection. You are neighbors with the Brannans and Lees.

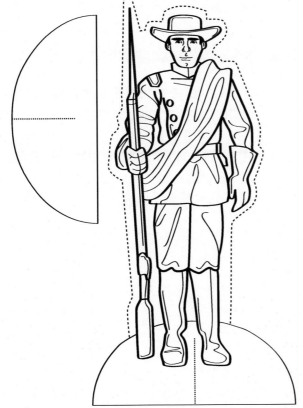

Confederate Horse Holders

When troops go into battle on foot, they need someone to hold their horses. You are members of the Confederate First Arkansas Cavalry under the command of General Cabell.

Fayetteville Characters *(cont.)*

Brannans

You are a good Fayetteville family, who own a nice house just north of the town's main intersection. You are neighbors with the Lees and Moores.

Lees

You are a good Fayetteville family, who own a nice house just north of the town's main intersection. You are neighbors with the Brannans and Moores.

Fayetteville Characters *(cont.)*

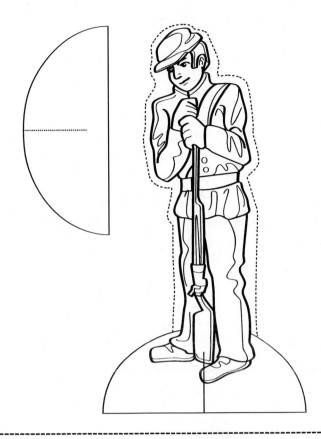

Confederate Skirmishers

You are members of the Confederate army under the command of General Cabell. Your job is to fight on foot and carry old duck-hunting guns that fire lead BB's.

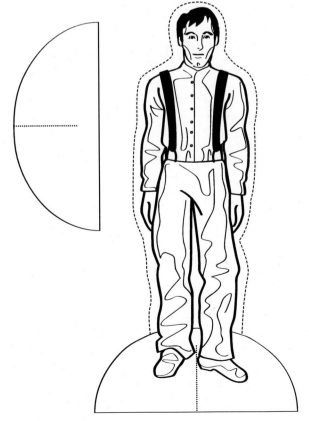

Union Soldiers Without Uniforms

You are Union soldiers under the command of Colonel Harrison, but there aren't enough uniforms to go around, and you haven't received one yet. Only a few of you even have boots or guns.

Fayetteville Characters *(cont.)*

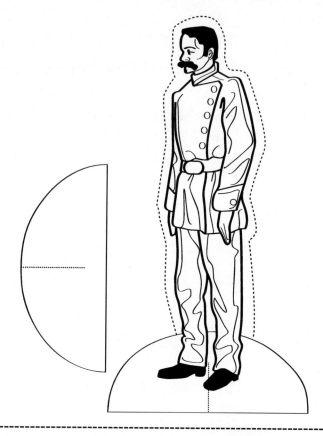

Major Ezra Fitch

You are a major in the Union army under the command of Colonel Harrison. You are embarrassed about the cowardly retreat of your army in the past and have promised not to retreat again.

Union Troops

You are soldiers in the Union army under the command of Colonel Harrison.

Fayetteville Characters *(cont.)*

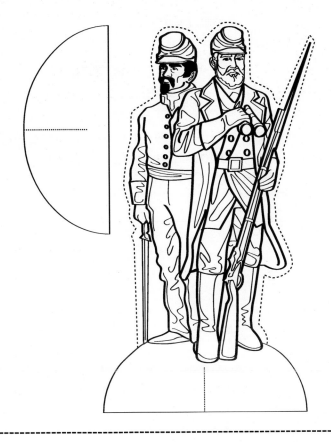

Confederate Troops

You are soldiers in the Confederate army under the command of General Cabell.

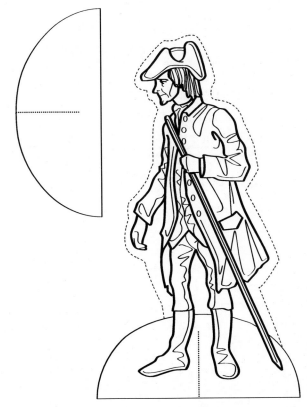

Ben Davis

You live in Fayetteville with your brother's family, and sometimes have problems understanding things. Your brother is a Confederate soldier and is away fighting the Civil War.

Fayetteville Characters *(cont.)*

First Confederate Arkansas Cavalry

You are soldiers in the Confederate army under the command of General Cabell.

Dr. Carpenter

You are a doctor for the Union army under the command of Colonel Harrison, but you feel that any wounded soldier deserves the best care you can give.

Building Fayetteville

1. Choose three or four artists to use pencils to enlarge the Fayetteville map on your town surface. They should draw the roads first.

2. Work with classmates to cut out, color, and glue together model buildings.

3. Paint or color the ground of your town (use different colors for forests, fields, and for the city).

4. Label all model buildings and glue them in their CORRECT places.

5. Don't forget to create the models of your characters!

Fayetteville Map

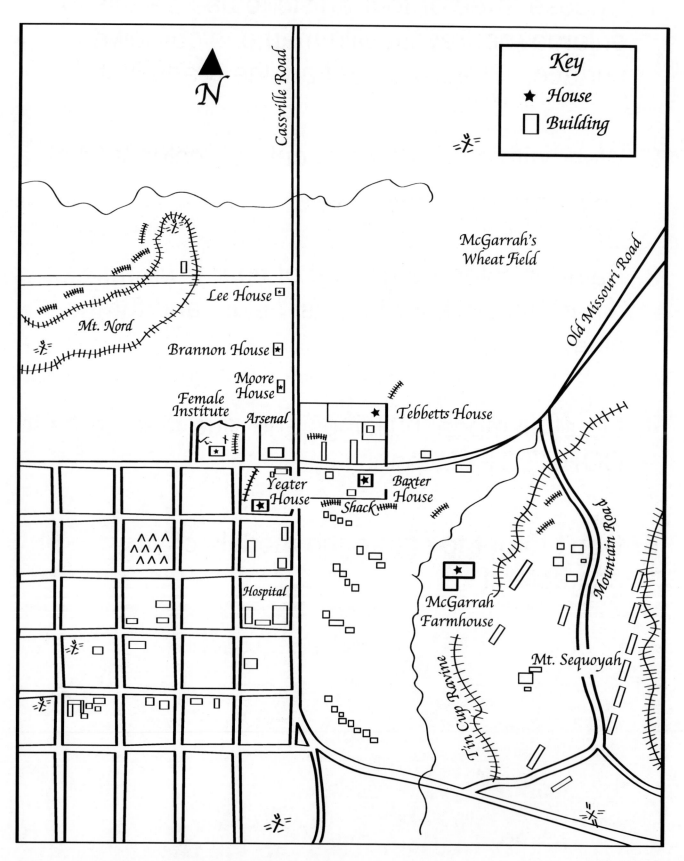

Building Template

Directions: Cut along the solid lines and fold along the dotted lines to make a building.

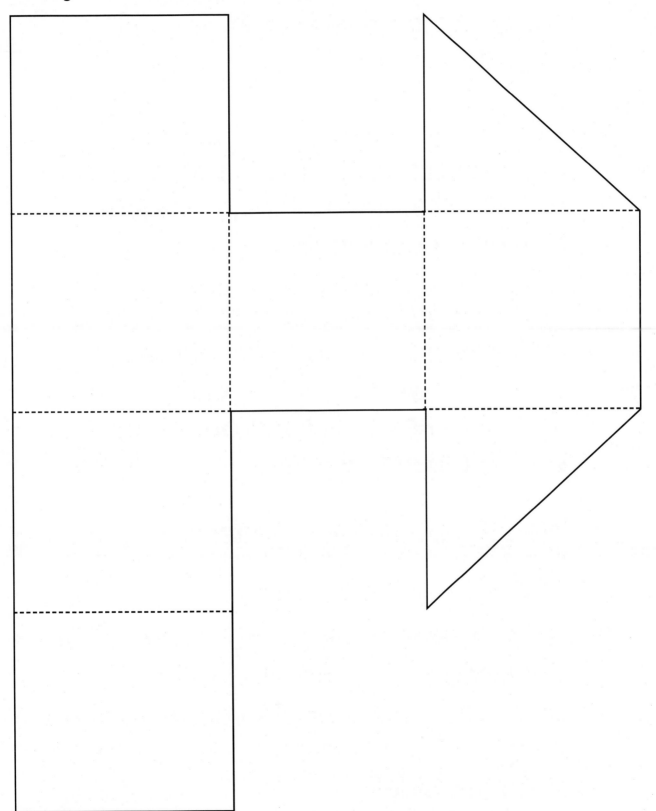

Habits of Mind Discussion

1. Who do you think was a better leader, Colonel Harrison or General Cabell?

2. What do you think was the most important factor in the Battle of Fayetteville (technology, decisions, bravery, luck, etc.)?

3. The Civil War was one of the first in the world in which civilians were killed. Do you think it is easier or harder to keep civilians out of harm's way in today's wars?

4. Was the Battle of Fayetteville worth fighting?

5. What do you think it would have been like living in Fayetteville during the Civil War? How would you have liked living next to people who fought for the other side?

Expansion and the Oregon Trail

Overview

Working in small groups, students will follow the Oregon Trail from St. Louis to the rich soils of the Willamette Valley. In a choose-your-own adventure format, groups will have to make decisions along the way. Make a wrong choice and the group could be waylaid by any number of hazards. This activity explores the realities and hardships of westward expansion while providing a geographical overview of the mid-nineteenth century push toward the far coast.

The total class time to complete the activity should be about three, 50-minute periods. You will measure student learning through discussion and evaluation of game activities.

Inside of a pioneer wagon
Source: The National Archives

Objectives

- Examine, interpret, and analyze physical and cultural patterns and their interactions, such as land use, settlement patterns, cultural transmission of customs and ideas, and ecosystem changes. (NCSS)
- Students will gain an experiential overview of life on, and the culture of, the Oregon Trail.

Materials

- copies of reproducibles (pages 141–155) as described on page 130
- ±100 straws or short sticks
- hat or box to draw for student names

Expansion and the Oregon Trail *(cont.)*

Preparation

Total preparation time should be about 20 minutes. Ask a parent volunteer to help with the copying before you begin the activity.

1. Write each student's name on a slip of paper and place all slips in a hat or box, called the Chance Hat. You will draw names from this hat to see which pioneers die of chance occurrences along the trail.

2. Make one copy per group of each of the following sheets:
   - *Supplies Information Sheet* (page 141)
   - *Pioneer Group Stats* (page 142)
   - *Pioneer Money* (page 143)

3. Make 10 copies of the *Decision Cards* (pages 144–154).

4. Make an overhead transparency of the *Habits of Mind Discussion* (page 155) to use at the conclusion of the activity.

Directions

1. Read the *Introduction Read-Aloud* (page 131) to the students.

2. Divide the class into groups of three. Each group will role-play a wagon train trying to travel from St. Louis to the Willamette Valley in Oregon.

3. Give each group a copy of the *Supplies Information Sheet*, *Pioneer Group Stats*, and *Pioneer Money*.

4. Start reading the *Oregon Trail Choose-Your-Own-Adventure Script* (pages 132–140). Notes to you, for the smooth running of the game, are italicized within the script.

5. At various points along the way, groups will need to make decisions. Based on each decision, you will give groups one of two activity sheets—groups who make the "good" decision will play a pioneer game. Those who choose poorly will be penalized on their *Pioneer Group Stats* sheet and will need to answer five questions correctly before you restart the narrative. This will take 5–10 minutes depending on class skill. Groups will bring their finished questions to you. You can check their answers using the key on page 140. Mark any incorrect answers and ask students to revise their choices. If students are not able to answer the questions correctly in your given time, you will penalize them another week on their *Pioneer Group Stats* sheet. The script will walk you through decisions and consequences with little headache.

6. If a group cannot pay needed money, are delayed by six weeks, or if all group members die, then the group fails to reach Oregon (most groups will survive). Depending on your class, you may have the members from "dead" groups sit quietly or they may join other groups. The game is rigged such that groups will likely not die until near the end.

7. Read the *Closure Read-Aloud* (page 140) to the students and complete the *Habits of Mind Discussion* (page 155).

Expansion and the Oregon Trail *(cont.)*

Things to Consider

1. The *Supplies Information Sheet* is a bit mathematically challenging. Depending on your class, you may need to calculate the amount of needed supplies as a class. Once you have calculated the standard supplies, groups could still choose to scrimp or splurge where they see fit.

2. The game is rigged such that groups shouldn't die until near the end of the game; however, if a group is especially unlucky, you may want to have them take notes, or become advisors to other groups to avoid students sitting around with little to do.

3. Make sure you get a definite decision from each group before passing out decision sheets or otherwise tipping your hand as to the correct decision.

4. Groups are primarily on the honor system in marking their *Pioneer Group Stats* sheet. Make sure that groups are aware that if you catch them cheating (or if there is excessive talking) they will be penalized either in weeks, money, or lives.

5. If resources permit, you might want to use a pull-down or wall-mounted map of the United States to help students follow their progress across the Oregon Trail.

Introduction Read-Aloud

By the mid 1800s it was getting a bit crowded in the East, and people were starting to hear stories of a land far to the west that was so fertile you could drop a seed at your feet and it would grow corn nine-feet tall.

Unfortunately, some of these stories were not true. The road to Oregon was not paved with gold. In fact, it wasn't paved at all. The Oregon Trail was little more than a set of wagon ruts through hard ground. But without these ruts that led through a break in the Rocky Mountains called South Pass, many of the western states such as California, Oregon, Washington, and Nevada would likely be part of Mexico or Canada.

It was a gap through the Rocky Mountains that the Lewis and Clark expedition had failed to find, forcing them to eat their tallow (animal fat) candles in the middle of mountains as winter raged around them.

Don't let this happen to your wagon train! Today, we will be playing an Oregon Trail game. We will be forming groups of three and following a choose-your-own-adventure game that I will read out loud. If you make smart decisions, you might reach the paradise that is Oregon; make bad choices and you might end up as bones along the trail.

Expansion and the Oregon Trail *(cont.)*

Oregon Trail Choose-Your-Own-Adventure Script

It's early April when your group of pioneers arrive in St. Louis, the starting point of the Oregon Trail. The snow is just melting from the nearby fields, but a cold wind still rips across the 2,000 miles you will need to travel before reaching Oregon. The mountains and high plains are still locked in ice. It's a few weeks before you will need to yoke oxen to your small wagon, load your supplies in the back, and be on your way. Before then, there's much to do.

The first part of the trail is actually a boat ride, 200 miles west on the Missouri River. Enjoy this part of your journey, because it will be the easiest by far. While you're on the boat, you will need to choose what supplies to buy with the $250 you were able to scrape together. Don't spend all your money, because you might need some along the way. However, remember that supplies along the trail can be a bit more expensive, if you can find them at all. Take 10 minutes to explore your *Supplies Information Sheet* and write down how you will spend your money. This is your only chance to buy supplies before you leave! Choose well!

Allow 10 minutes for students to complete the Supplies Information Sheet.

There are a couple of towns called "jumping off" points that pioneers use to buy supplies before hitting the trail. The most popular towns are Independence, St. Joseph, Westport, Omaha, and Council Bluffs. Each of these towns depends on the spring boom in sales to bring in enough money to survive the rest of the year. On the boat from St. Louis, you hear a pioneer in a tattered leather hat named William Rothwell talking about St. Joseph: "I have never in my life heard as many false statements as were told us in coming up here. We were frequently told that at least 15 to 20 cases of cholera were dying daily in St. Joseph."

Each town has paid people to say bad things about the other jumping off points, hoping to scare more pioneers into their town. You decide not to trust everyone you meet on this journey.

Like many pioneers, you choose to start your trek from Independence, Missouri, where you buy supplies and camp just out of town. There are over three square miles of people camped here, buying supplies and waiting for the right time to leave.

When will your wagon train choose to set out? As you see people starting to pack up their gear, the first decision you need to make is whether or not to try to leave just ahead of the crowd.

Decision 1: Do you decide to leave before the crowd?

Ask students to make Decision 1. Wait until each group has clearly stated its choice before distributing the Decision Cards. *(Yes is page 144. No is page 145.) Allow 5–10 minutes for completion of the decision activities. Then continue reading.*

Expansion and the Oregon Trail *(cont.)*

Oregon Trail Choose-Your-Own-Adventure Script *(cont.)*

Hopefully you decided to wait for a bit. There's not enough grass yet on the prairie to feed your hungry oxen, and you can't carry enough food to feed them from the wagon. There's a reason the crowd waited. Without grass, your oxen could starve and without oxen, you're stuck!

With the spring thaw, your wagon train sets out from Independence, loaded down with supplies. It's tough going and most of the time you can only travel at about two miles per hour. You could walk much faster. You know that if you don't reach Oregon by October, you will be unable to cross the mountain passes. If only it weren't for all the weight you have to carry! In fact, if you bought over 600 lbs. of flour, 450 lbs. of bacon, 30 lbs. of coffee, 60 lbs. of sugar, and 30 lbs. of salt, all you did is slow yourself down. Before you are 20 miles out of Independence, you decide the weight is just too much and you ditch the extra supplies by the roadside. Erase these extra amounts of supplies from your *Supplies Information Sheet.* Try not to waste any more money, or you might not make it to Oregon!

After about a week of traveling, you reach the popular campsite called Alcove Spring. As one pioneer describes it, "About three-fourths of a mile from our camp, we found a large spring of water, as cold and pure as if it had just been melted from ice. We named this Alcove Spring."

You have been drinking mud puddles and coffee for a week and would enjoy drinking your fill from Alcove Spring's clear waters, but you are also in the middle of American Indian territory, with the Cheyenne to the north and the Pawnee to the south. Do you stop to rest at the Springs, or do you continue on, fearful of the American Indians?

Decision 2: Do you camp at Alcove Springs or move as quickly as possible through American Indian territory?

Ask students to make Decision 2. Wait until each group has clearly stated its choice before distributing the Decision Cards. *(Camp at Alcove Spring is page 146. Keep Moving is page 147.) Allow 5–10 minutes for completion of the decision activities. Then continue reading.*

I hope you chose to stay at Alcove Springs for a bit. Your oxen needed a rest and there are many more dangerous things on the Oregon Trail than American Indians, who were usually very helpful. Bad drinking water killed many more settlers than did American Indians. In fact, more pioneers died from being accidentally shot than died in battles.

Expansion and the Oregon Trail *(cont.)*

Oregon Trail Choose-Your-Own-Adventure Script *(cont.)*

From Alcove Springs, you continue west, though I'll bet you could have guessed that. Already, your shoes are starting to wear thin. Some people will be walking the next 1,500 miles barefoot. At Rock Creek Station, the owner charges you one dollar to use his bridge. Pay this amount to your teacher at this time. I hope you're not getting low on cash; it'll take a lot more to make it all the way to Oregon.

In late May, you pass through Fort Kearny, which you hoped would be better. It's little more than a clump of sod buildings, a far cry from what you consider a fort. You decide not to expect much in the way of civilization along the rest of the trail. Unfortunately, one of you has just fallen off the wagon and been crushed by the wheels.

Draw a name from your Chance Hat to see which one student dies. The affected group should cross this student off their Pioneer Group Stats *sheet. This student can now be your assistant.*

You have been following the south side of the Platte River for hundreds of miles when you come to a point where the river widens and gets shallower. The majority of the tire ruts that you have been following end at the river's edge. You look across and it's hard to see the other side. It's at least a mile across, maybe more, but it doesn't look to be more than a foot or two deep. Do you cross the Platte River here, or do you continue following the south side?

Decision 3: Do you cross the Platte River where it is wide and looks shallow, or do you leave the wheel ruts and continue to follow the south bank?

Ask students to make Decision 3. Wait until each group has clearly stated its choice before distributing the Decision Cards. *(Cross the River is page 148. Follow South Bank is page 149.) Allow 5–10 minutes for completion of the decision activities. Then continue reading.*

Well, I hope you didn't decide to leave the wheel ruts. Off the Oregon Trail in every direction is unexplored land, full of dangers and delays. If you continued to follow the south bank, you found nowhere to cross and ended up following the South Platte to a dead end in Colorado, wasting time. Don't waste too much time or you'll be stuck somewhere along the trail when the next winter hits!

You are now in western Nebraska, though it's not a state yet. After spending weeks on the featureless plains, it's nice to finally come across some landmarks. First, you come to Courthouse Rock, then to the towering Chimney Rock, and finally to Scotts Bluff.

Expansion and the Oregon Trail *(cont.)*

Oregon Trail Choose-Your-Own-Adventure Script *(cont.)*

Scotts Bluff was described by the pioneer Thomas Eastin as follows:

> How can I describe the scene that now bursts upon us? Tower, bastion, dome and battlement vie in all their majesty before us. A dark cloud is rising in the northwest. A more beautiful and majestic scene cannot be conceived. How wonderful, how great, how sublime are Thy works, O God!

During this time, two of you die of accidental gunshot wounds.

> *Have your student assistant draw two names from your* Chance Hat *to see which students die. The affected group(s) should cross the student(s) off their* Pioneer Group Stats *sheet. These students now have to observe the game quietly. They can't talk to their group, but they can write down notes that share ideas about the future decisions.*

Just before reaching Scotts Bluff, the tire ruts split. It looks like the old trail goes around the south of the mountains, but a new set of wheel ruts cut through Scotts Bluff at a point called Mitchell Pass. In the soft sandstone rock, there are places where these new ruts cut eight feet into the stone! Which way do you go?

Decision 4: Do you take the new path through Mitchell Pass, or take the old route that cuts around the south end of Scotts Bluff?

> *Ask students to make Decision 4. Wait until each group has clearly stated its choice. Then keep reading because there are not any* Decision Cards *to distribute at this point.*

Though the trail through Mitchell Pass is shorter, it is also more treacherous. Groups that choose to go around the south end of Scotts Bluff rejoin the main train without incident. The groups that cut through Mitchell Pass, struggle with their wagons and oxen over the uneven terrain. On one particularly steep slope, a wagon gets away, crushing one pioneer.

> *Have your student assistant draw names from your* Chance Hat *to until he or she pulls the name of a student who chose to go over Mitchell Pass. The affected group should cross this student off their* Pioneer Group Stats *sheet. This student now has to observe the game quietly. He or she can't talk to his or her group but can write down notes.*

Due to the rough going you rejoin the main trail at about the same time as the pioneers that chose to take the longer route to the south. You are now in Wyoming . . . "where seldom is heard a discouraging word and the skies . . ." Well, I'll bet you can guess what the skies are like. It's a beautiful late-June morning when you reach Fort Laramie, which you can hear from a mile off and smell from even further. After being on the trail for a couple months, you're not used to the squawk of chickens and the odor of people living together.

Expansion and the Oregon Trail *(cont.)*

Oregon Trail Choose-Your-Own-Adventure Script *(cont.)*

You've been looking forward to Fort Laramie for quite some time. The chest of drawers your great grandfather made is pretty, but it's just weighing you down. You hauled the drawers this far in hopes that you could sell them in Fort Laramie. It turns out that buying and selling is a little different than what you are used to in the East. Nobody wants to buy a set of drawers. Most everybody in this town is a pioneer and they don't want the extra weight any more than you do. What people do want are supplies.

Look at your *Supplies Information Sheet*. If your group bought less than 600 lbs. of flour, 450 lbs. of bacon, 30 lbs. of coffee, 60 lbs. of sugar, and 30 lbs. of salt, you will need to resupply your stores to get to these amounts. Remember how much these cost at your jumping off point of Independence? Well, they are a little more expensive in Fort Laramie. One pioneer named James Clyman reported, "Groceries and liquors exhorbitantly high. For instance, sugar $1.50 per pint or cupful. Flour $1 per pint."

For every type of provision that is below the amount that you should have bought at the beginning, you need to pay $5 to restock. For example, if my group had purchased too little bacon and too little salt, I would have to pay $10. Remember, you should have 600 lbs. of flour, 450 lbs. of bacon, 30 lbs. of coffee, 60 lbs. of sugar, and 30 lbs. of salt. If you don't have enough money, you will need to turn around and go back to St. Louis or stay in Fort Laramie.

Allow students a minute or two to pay for supplies. They should update their Supplies Information Sheets *and pay you. If you catch groups cheating, penalize them at least $10.*

After leaving Fort Laramie, a little lighter in the pockets as well as in the wagon, you pass by another fort, called Fort Casper. This fort is the sight of a popular river crossing. Pay $1 for the ferryboat.

Collect $1 from each group.

Though the Oregon Trail is difficult, it's not all hard work; sometimes there's a chance to have some fun! Your wagon train spends the Fourth of July camped at Independence Rock with a number of other pioneers. You all bake fresh pies and carve your names in the stone. A pioneer named Margaret Hecox described the celebration saying, "Being the Fourth of July, we concluded to lay by and celebrate the day. The children had no fireworks, but we all joined in singing patriotic songs and shared in a picnic lunch."

Expansion and the Oregon Trail *(cont.)*

Oregon Trail Choose-Your-Own-Adventure Script *(cont.)*

Children also played a game using dried buffalo chips. Who would like to explain to the class what a buffalo chip is? These chips were an important resource for pioneers who used them mostly as fuel for campfires. There weren't enough trees along the trail to use for wood. During this time, one person dies from a bear attack.

Have your student assistant draw a name from your Chance Hat to see which student dies. The affected group should cross this student off their Pioneer Group Stats *sheet. This student now has to observe the game quietly. He or she can't talk to his or her group but can write down notes.*

Your wagon train has now come to the most important point on the entire Oregon Trail: South Pass. It is this pass through the Rocky Mountains that made westward expansion possible. South Pass is the only point along the entire stretch of the Rocky Mountains through which you could drive a wagon, and it was found only by luck. A group of explorers called the Astorians had capsized their canoe on the Snake River and by the time they thrashed through the mountains to the West Coast, they were in big trouble. It was on the trip back east for help that Robert Stuart found the 20-mile-wide South Pass.

Congratulations! You are now in Oregon Country! However, three people die of cholera.

Have your student assistant draw three names from your Chance Hat to see which students die. The affected groups should cross the names off their Pioneer Group Stats *sheet. These students now have to observe the game quietly. They can't talk to their groups but can write down notes.*

You now have a choice to make—do you stop your wagon train while your friends are dying of cholera and wait to give them a proper burial, or do you leave them by the side of the trail while they are still alive and continue on without them?

Decision 5: Do you wait for people to die of cholera and then give them a proper burial, or do you just leave them by the side of the trail?

Ask students to make Decision 5. Wait until each group has clearly stated its choice before distributing the Decision Cards. *(Wait is page 150. Keep Moving is page 151.) Allow 5–10 minutes for completion of the decision activities. Then continue reading.*

It was important to keep moving on the Oregon Trail. A delay of two weeks to wait for a pioneer to die of cholera could be the difference between one person dying and the entire group dying from an early winter on the trail.

Expansion and the Oregon Trail *(cont.)*

Oregon Trail Choose-Your-Own-Adventure Script *(cont.)*

Remember that "Congratulations, you are now in Oregon Country" part? Well, it's true that you are in Oregon Country, but you are still a long ways from the end of your journey in the Willamette Valley. In fact, you have the two most dangerous decisions of the entire trip still in front of you.

You have come to the Three Island Crossing of the Snake River. Here's what happened to the pioneer Samuel Hancock at this crossing, "We lost two of our men, Ayres and Stringer. Ayres got into trouble with his mules in crossing the stream. Stringer, who was about 30, went to his relief, and both were drowned in sight of their women folks. The bodies were never recovered." Your only other choice is to stay on the south side of the river, traveling far out of your way. What do you do?

Decision 6: Do you cross the Snake River at Three River Crossing or do you detour, staying on the south side of the river?

Ask students to make Decision 6. Wait until each group has clearly stated its choice. Then keep reading because there are not any Decision Cards *to distribute at this point.*

The people who decide to ford the Snake River at Three Island Crossing get lucky! Nobody is hurt and you get across without incident. If you decided to stay on the south side of the river, you wasted one full week. Cross this week off your *Pioneer Group Stats* sheet. Remember, if you're not in the Willamette Valley by November, you may end up in serious trouble.

It's mid-September as you pass through Fort Boise on the west side of the Rocky Mountains, and the chill in the air even at lower altitudes is starting to hint that fall is on the way. The first encouraging sight you see is the Grande Ronde Valley, green fertile land that pushes up against the mountain walls. This is what Captain Benjamin Bonneville said about the Grande Ronde:

> Its sheltered situation, embosomed in mountains, renders it good pasturing ground in the winter time; when the elk come down to it in great numbers, driven out of the mountains by the snow. The Indians then resort to it to hunt. They likewise come to it in the summer to dig the camash root, of which it produces immense quantities. When this plant is in blossom, the whole valley is tinted by its blue flowers, and looks like the ocean when overcast by a cloud.

Still, the Grande Ronde was a wild place without settlement or exploration, and you decide to push on to the Willamette Valley, where you have heard there is civilization.

Expansion and the Oregon Trail *(cont.)*

Oregon Trail Choose-Your-Own-Adventure Script *(cont.)*

It's now late September. The days are starting to shorten, the nights are cold, and you are starting to get a bit worried about the changing seasons. You're sick of the trail and ready to be in the Willamette Valley. Unfortunately, the most dangerous part of your trip is just around the corner.

Just ahead, at the Dalles, the Columbia River is squeezed into raging whitewater by narrow mountain cliffs. Here's how the pioneer Parthenia Blank described it:

> The appearance of the river here changes—and from being a rapid, shallow and narrow stream, it becomes a wide, deep and still one, in some places more than a mile wide and too deep to be sounded. The banks are precipitous and rocky, and several hundred feet high in some places.

Here is where the wagon tracks you've been following end. Later, Sam Barlow would cut a path around the rapids, but for now, the only way through the Cascade Mountains is to float your wagons down the Columbia River. You've come too far to turn around. This is what happened to Lindsey Applegate:

> One of our boats, containing six persons, was caught in one of those terrible whirlpools and upset. My son, ten years old, my brother Jesse's son Edward, same age, were lost. It was a painful scene beyond description. We dared not go to their assistance without exposing the occupants of the other boat to certain destruction. The bodies of the drowned were never recovered.

There are two options for making the Columbia River just a bit safer, book a commercial ferry or hire a American Indian guide. The ferry costs $25, and a guide costs $10.

Decision 7: Cross the Columbia alone, on a ferry ($25), or with an American Indian guide ($10)?

Ask students to make Decision 7. Wait until each group has clearly stated its choice before distributing the Decision Cards. *(Alone is page 152. On a Ferry is page 153. American Indian Guide is page 154.) Allow 5–10 minutes for completion of the decision activities. Then continue reading.*

Sometimes the most expensive option is not the best. While pioneers were more likely to trust a ferryboat, they were way overpriced and usually overbooked. Because pioneers sometimes had to wait for weeks before there was space on a ferry, a town developed at the Dalles. Whichever method you choose to cross the Columbia, it's risky. Many didn't make it. But it was the last hurdle on the Oregon Trail!

Expansion and the Oregon Trail *(cont.)*

Oregon Trail Choose-Your-Own-Adventure Script *(cont.)*

You are now really in Oregon Country! Here's how James Miller described Oregon City, "On our arrival in Oregon City, I found everything quite different from what I expected. There were three small churches, three stores, two blacksmiths shops, two flour mills and one weekly newspaper, the *Oregon Spectator*."

Upon arriving in Oregon City, each male pioneer was allowed 640 acres of prime farmland and people spread out from the city in all directions to stake their claims. To each group with at least one living pioneer—welcome to Oregon and the farmland of your dreams!

Closure Read-Aloud

The Oregon Trail was like a shooting star. At first there was nothing but waving grass and open plains, then all of a sudden wagon trains stretched across almost the entire route, towns sprang up like prairie grass, and every eastern farmer with a twinkle in his eye was hot to strike it rich in the new land out west. And then within the short span of 25 years, railroad tracks were laid down and the days of the Oregon Trail itself were over. But before this shooting star burned itself out, more than 500,000 people made the journey across the country, and the Wild West was just a little bit tamer.

As you saw, for those hardy souls that made the journey by wagon train, life was far from easy. In real life, one in ten died along the way, and many walked the 2,000 miles barefoot. But the payoff was worth the trip. Some struck gold in California, others struck black gold in the form of rich farmland in Oregon's Willamette Valley, and all had the adventure of a lifetime!

Answer Key

Use this sheet to quickly check the multiple-choice questions from each "wrong" decision sheet. If there are incorrect answers, mark them and ask students to revise their choices. If a group is unable to find the five correct answers before your given time, you may penalize them an additional week to be marked on their *Pioneer Group Stats* sheet.

Decision Card #1: (page 144)	1. b	2. c	3. b	4. d	5. b
Decision Card #2: (page 147)	1. c	2. b	3. a	4. c	5. c
Decision Card #3: (page 149)	1. c	2. d	3. b	4. c	5. c
Decision Card #5: (page 150)	1. c	2. d	3. b	4. a	5. c
Decision Card #7: (pages 152–153)	1. b	2. a	3. d	4. c	5. a

Supplies Information Sheet

Directions: Before you begin the Oregon Trail, you will need to buy supplies in the town of Independence. This will be the most inexpensive place to buy supplies, and the only sure place to find everything you need. However, if you overload your wagon, you might not make it far enough to worry about supplies, and if you spend all your money now, you'll never make it to Oregon.

- **Every month**, each person needs 40 lbs. of flour, 30 lbs. of bacon, 2 lbs. of coffee, 4 lbs. of sugar, and 2 lbs. of salt.

- You will be on the Oregon Trail for about **5 months**.

- How much of each supply will you need for **3 people**?

- You have **$245** to spend. If you haven't already cut out your money sheet, do so now.

- You also need a farm wagon, two oxen, cooking supplies, a tent and bedding, hunting supplies, and a package of general gear that covers everything from tools, to a water barrel, to harnesses for the oxen.

- Use the chart below to spend your money. The flour is done for you. Notice that you have bought 6 barrels of flour for a total cost of $24 and a total weight of 600 pounds.

Once you have chosen what to buy, show this list to your teacher and give him or her the correct amount of money.

Item	Cost	#	$	Total weight
100 lbs. barrel of flour	$4	6	$24	600 lbs.
50 lbs. of bacon	$2			
10 lbs. of coffee	$1			
10 lbs. of sugar	$1.50			
10 lbs. of salt	$1			
1 ox	$30			N/A
1 farm wagon	$50			N/A
cooking supplies (15 lbs.)	$5			
tent and bedding (20 lbs.)	$5			
hunting supplies (20 lbs.)	$10			
general supplies (200 lbs.)	$15			
Totals:				

Pioneer Group Stats

Penalty Weeks

As we read the story, cross off one week below for every extra week you are delayed. If you cross off all six weeks, you are stranded on the Oregon Trail.

1	2	3	4	5	6

Pioneers Alive

Write your name below one of these boxes and draw a quick picture of yourself as a pioneer. If you die, you will put an "X" through your pioneer box.

Pioneer Money

Directions: Cut out the money to use on your journey.

Fifty **50** Dollars	Fifty **50** Dollars
Twenty **20** Dollars	Twenty **20** Dollars
Twenty **20** Dollars	Twenty **20** Dollars
Twenty **20** Dollars	Ten **10** Dollars
Ten **10** Dollars	Five **5** Dollars
Five **5** Dollars	Five **5** Dollars
Five **5** Dollars	One **1** Dollar
One **1** Dollar	One **1** Dollar
One **1** Dollar	One **1** Dollar

Decision Cards

Decision #1: Do you decide to leave before the crowd?

Yes

Unfortunately, you left too early and the prairie grass hasn't sprouted yet. Your oxen have nothing to eat.

- Cross off one week on your *Pioneer Group Stats* sheet as you waste time returning to Independence for more supplies.
- Pay your teacher $15 for these extra supplies.

Directions: Answer the questions below and then show them to your teacher. If you have wrong answers, you will need to try again. Find all the correct answers within five minutes, or you will waste another week!

1. What is the strongest animal used for pulling covered wagons?

   a. horses   b. oxen   c. mules   d. cows

2. In which time period was the Oregon Trail most used?

   a. 1610–1776   b. 1776–1812   c. 1836–1869   d. 1875–1910

3. Which of the following was the MOST dangerous to pioneers?

   a. American Indian attack   c. cold winters
   b. cholera   d. starvation

4. Some pioneers traveled in search of gold, which was found where?

   a. Washington   b. Oregon   c. Idaho   d. California

5. What was the name of the important pass through the Rocky Mountains?

   a. Lolo Pass   b. South Pass   c. Indiana   d. Mitchell Pass

---

Decision Cards *(cont.)*

Decision #1: Do you decide to leave before the crowd?

No

Good choice! By the time you decide to leave, the prairie is covered in green grass, which provides food for your oxen. While the other groups are struggling to catch up, play the pioneer game below.

Poor Doggie

1. Form a circle with the other groups who chose to wait for the crowd.

2. One person will be the doggie and will go around the circle trying to make people laugh by pretending to be a dog. The doggie may whine, bark, and PRETEND to lick people.

3. The people in the circle must pet the dog and say "poor doggie, poor doggie, etc."

4. If someone laughs, they become the doggie.

Decision Cards *(cont.)*

Decision #2: Do you camp at Alcove Springs or move as quickly as possible through American Indian territory?

Camp at Alcove Spring

Good decision! Contrary to popular belief, attacks from American Indians were only a small risk on the Oregon Trail and were much less dangerous than drinking unclean water! Instead of getting sick to your stomach like the other groups, play the pioneer game below.

Who Has the Button?

1. Form a circle with the other groups who chose to camp at Alcove Springs.

2. Find a button, pen cap, coin, or scrap of paper that you can easily hide in your hand.

3. One person will be "it." The "it" person closes his or her eyes while the rest of the group passes around your button.

4. The people in the circle all pretend they have the button.

5. Whoever is "it" gets two guesses to find the button. If they find the button, the person who had it is "it." If they do not guess where the button is, they will stay "it" for another round.

Decision Cards *(cont.)*

Decision #2: Do you camp at Alcove Springs or move as quickly as possible through American Indian territory?

Keep Moving

Oops! There are many more dangerous things on the Oregon Trail than American Indian attacks, and drinking dirty water is one of them.

- Cross off one week on your Pioneer Group Stats sheet as you waste time recovering from sickness.
- Also, pay your teacher $10 for stomach medicine. You're lucky to get it!

Directions: Answer the questions below and then show them to your teacher. If you have wrong answers, you will need to try again. Find all the correct answers within five minutes, or you will waste another week!

1. About how many months does it take to travel the Oregon Trail?

   a. two   b. three   c. five   d. seven

2. About how long is the Oregon Trail?

   a. 1,000 miles   b. 2,000 miles   c. 3,000 miles   d. 4,000 miles

3. What current state does the Oregon Trail **NOT** pass through?

   a. Texas   b. Wyoming   c. Nebraska   d. Colorado

4. What is the first step for most pioneers' journey west?

   a. take the train to Salt Lake City   c. buy supplies
   b. wait for the prairie grass to grow   d. reach Alcove Springs

5. What did pioneers hope to find in Oregon?

   a. gold   c. fertile land
   b. the Inside Passage   d. Mexico

Decision Cards *(cont.)*

Decision #3: Do you cross the Platte River, or do you leave the wheel ruts and continue to follow the south bank?

Cross the River

Good Choice! But sometimes even if you make all the best choices, the Oregon Trail can be difficult.

• Pay your teacher $5 for a replacement tent after yours falls out of the back of your wagon and is swept away in the river.

While the river crossing was difficult, at least it was quick. Play the pioneer game below while you wait for the other groups to catch up.

Hot and Cold

1. Get together with the other groups who chose to cross the Platte River.

2. Find a small object such as a pen cap or eraser that you can hide in the classroom.

3. The person who is "it" will cover his or her eyes and ears while the rest of the people hide the object somewhere in the classroom.

4. When the person who is "it" opens his or her eyes, the rest of the class will guide this person to the object by saying "hotter" and "colder."

5. Once the "it" person finds the object, it will be someone else's turn.

Decision Cards (cont.)

Decision #3: Do you cross the Platte River, or do you leave the wheel ruts and continue to follow the south bank?

Follow South Bank

Sometimes pioneers needed to take risks in order to save time. By continuing to follow the south bank of the Platte River, you end up dead-ending in Colorado and need to retrace your steps.

- Cross off two weeks on your *Pioneer Group Stats* sheet as you backtrack to the correct crossing.
- Pay your teacher $5 to replace a tent you lose during the crossing.

Directions: Answer the questions below and then show them to your teacher. If you have wrong answers, you will need to try again. Find all the correct answers within five minutes, or you will waste another week!

1. The majority of the Oregon Trail migration took place just before which war?

    a. War of 1812   b. World War I   c. Civil War   d. World War II

2. What did pioneers burn most in their campfires?

    a. wood   b. coal   c. white gas   d. buffalo chips

3. Which of the following is not considered a necessary pioneer supply?

    a. coffee   b. corn   c. bacon   d. flour

4. About how many miles did pioneers have to travel per day (2,000 miles in 5 months)?

    a. 3 miles   b. 6 miles   c. 13 miles   d. 20 miles

5. Why did people stop using the Oregon Trail in about 1869?

    a. the Pacific Ocean   c. Transcontinental Railway
    b. invention of the airplane   d. American Indian attacks

---

Decision Cards *(cont.)*

Decision #5: Do you wait for people to die of cholera, or do you keep moving?

Wait

The Oregon Trail is not always a nice place. By waiting for your fellow traveler to die of cholera, you have put the entire group in danger.

- Cross off two weeks on your *Pioneer Group Stats* sheet as you waste time waiting.

Directions: Answer the questions below and then show them to your teacher. If you have wrong answers, you will need to try again. Find all the correct answers within five minutes, or you will waste another week!

1. Who was the first U.S. group (early 1800s) to travel cross-country to the West Coast?

   a. the Astorians
   b. the Whitmans
   c. Lewis and Clark
   d. Pike and Long

2. About how many total pioneers traveled the Oregon Trail?

   a. 1,000   b. 10,000   c. 100,000   d. 500,000

3. South Pass was a 20-mile valley that runs through which mountain range?

   a. Cascades
   b. Rocky Mountains
   c. Appalachians
   d. Platte

4. Pioneers "circled their wagons" at night to prevent:

   a. their livestock from escaping.
   b. American Indian attack.
   c. their campfires being blown out.
   d. crop circles.

5. Which toy would a pioneer child **NOT** have had?

   a. rag doll   b. wooden toys   c. squirt gun   d. books

Decision Cards *(cont.)*

Decision #5: Do you wait for people to die of cholera, or do you keep moving?

Keep Moving

You decide to keep the wagons moving but leave a watcher with the dying person. Your watcher is able to catch up later, without costing the group any time. Play the pioneer game below while waiting for the other groups to catch up.

Jack Straws

1. Stay in your own, three-person group and get a pile of straws from your teacher.

2. Pile the straws in the middle of your group.

3. Take turns trying to take a straw out of the pile without moving any of the other straws.

4. If you move any straws but the one you are taking from the pile, you are out.

Decision Cards *(cont.)*

Decision #7: Cross the Columbia alone, on a ferry ($25), or with an American Indian guide ($10)?

Alone

Wow, your group must really be strapped for cash. Crossing the Columbia on your own means building a raft and floating the dangerous rapids without help.

- One pioneer falls off the raft and dies. Cross off one person from your *Pioneer Group Stats* sheet.
- Cross off one week on your *Pioneer Group Stats* sheet as you struggle to build a raft.
- Pay your teacher $5 for building supplies.

Directions: Answer the questions below and then show them to your teacher. If you have wrong answers, you will need to try again. Find all the correct answers within five minutes, or you will waste another week!

1. Where did pioneers cross the Columbia River?

   a. Falls   b. Dalles   c. Portage   d. Three Islands

2. What was the area of Oregon that most pioneers wanted to reach?

   a. Willamette Valley   c. Gold Rush
   b. Cascade Range   d. West Coast

3. What would be likely dates for starting and ending the Oregon Trail?

   a. June 1, October 1   c. March 20, July 20
   b. May 15, September 1   d. May 1, November 1

4. A pioneer who had never farmed before was known as:

   a. buzzard bait   b. a newbie   c. a greenhorn   d. a cowpuncher

5. Winter was dangerous to travelers on the Oregon Trail because of:

   a. blizzards in the mountains.   c. tired animals.
   b. heat stroke.   d. rain on the plains.

Decision Cards *(cont.)*

Decision #7: Cross the Columbia alone, on a ferry ($25), or with an American Indian guide ($10)?

On a Ferry

Many pioneers wanted to take the ferry across the Columbia, and there was frequently a long wait. Most also thought the ferries were way overpriced. A ferry across the river could make as much as $2,000 per day!

- Cross off two weeks on your *Pioneer Group Stats* sheet as you wait for a ferry ride.
- Pay your teacher $25 for a ferry ticket.

Directions: Answer the questions below and then show them to your teacher. If you have wrong answers, you will need to try again. Find all the correct answers within five minutes, or you will waste another week!

1. Where did pioneers cross the Columbia River?

   a. Falls   b. Dalles   c. Portage   d. Three Islands

2. What was the area of Oregon that most pioneers wanted to reach?

   a. Willamette Valley   c. Gold Rush
   b. Cascade Range   d. West Coast

3. What would be likely dates for starting and ending the Oregon Trail?

   a. June 1, October 1   c. March 20, July 20
   b. May 15, September 1   d. May 1, November 1

4. A pioneer who had never farmed before was known as:

   a. buzzard bait   b. a newbie   c. a greenhorn   d. a cowpuncher

5. Winter was dangerous to travelers on the Oregon Trail because of:

   a. blizzards in the mountains.   c. tired animals.
   b. heat stroke.   d. rain on the plains.

Decision Cards (cont.)

Decision #7: Cross the Columbia alone, on a ferry ($25), or with an American Indian guide ($10)?

American Indian Guide

Congratulations! This is the quickest and most cost-effective way across the Columbia River. Here's what pioneer Overton Johnson had to say about the American Indian guides: "It requires the most dexterous management, which these wild navigators are masters of, to pass the dreadful chasm in safety. A single stroke amiss, would be inevitable destruction."

• Pay your teacher $10 for guide fees.

Instead of struggling to get across the Columbia River, play the pioneer game below while you wait for the other groups.

Ducks Fly

1. Get together with the other groups who chose to cross with an American Indian guide.

2. One leader will say things like "ducks fly" and then flap his or her arms; the rest of the group will copy this action. The leader might also say "ducks quack" or "pigs oink."

3. The leader may also say things that don't make sense, like "ducks moo."

4. If any people in the group copy an action that doesn't make sense, they are out.

Habits of Mind Discussion

1. What ideas did you have about the Oregon Trail before this game that you found out were different than you thought?

2. What do you think would have been the most difficult part of traveling on the Oregon Trail?

3. If you could bring one modern item with you on the Oregon Trail, what would it be?

4. Do you think you would have chosen to migrate west on the Oregon Trail, or would you have stayed in the East? Why?

5. How do you think families felt when they started the journey? Compare this feeling with the thought of taking a trip across the country today.

Immigration, Industry, and the American Dream

Overview

In this game, formatted as a mystery party, students will role-play representative figures of the immigration boom and second industrial revolution (1850–1920). Some, like Andrew Carnegie, are famous figures from United States history, while others will represent recent immigrants. Students have scripted questions, answers, and clues to use while trying to solve the "Mystery of the Golden Key." This fun game provides an overview of period issues and attitudes while offering students the opportunity to express their inner hams. Depending on your desired level of involvement, you can run this game with very little prep, or can have students dress up, bring food, and have a well-planned class party.

The total class time to complete the activity should be about two, 50-minute periods. You will assess student learning through discussion and by collecting their finished character sheets at the end of the activity.

Political cartoon showing Andrew Carnegie
donating his money
Source: The Library of Congress

Objectives

- Students will describe the way national/cultural roots affect individual development. (NCSS)
- Students will meet the personalities that shaped the early 1900s and will experience the contrasting viewpoints of industry vs. unions and immigrations vs. xenophobia.

Materials

- copies of reproducibles (pages 160–174) as described below

- index cards
- colored markers

Preparation

Total preparation time should be about 15 minutes.

1. Make one copy of the *Crime Scene Report* (page 160) for Inspector Jones.

2. Make a copy of the *Guest List* (page 161) for each student.

3. Make two copies of the *Character Sheets* (page 162–173).

4. Make an overhead of the *Habits of Mind Discussion* (page 174).

Immigration, Industry, and the American Dream *(cont.)*

Directions

1. You will be the host of this mystery party. There are 12 characters for the party. In most classrooms, you will need to divide the class in half and have two different parties running at the same time. Make sure you have a physical barrier in the room (a row of desks) so that students only talk to the characters at their own party.

2. Distribute the *Guest List* and assign students to the characters they will be role-playing. If your class has more than 24 students, you will have to ask a few students to share characters. You can call them twins.

3. Distribute the *Character Sheets* and give students time to make themselves nametags. If you like, you can assign this for homework and ask students to come to class with costumes as well. You may also want to give your students a day to study their *Character Sheets* to prepare for the party.

4. At the beginning of your mystery day, greet characters, check for nametags, and then read the *Introduction Read-Aloud* (page 158) to the students.

5. Remind students that their primary goal is to ask characters questions as directed on their *Character Sheets*. They should record the characters' answers because these are the clues to the mystery. Only through talking to other characters will they be able to figure out the solution to the mystery.

6. Students may also gather additional clues, which they should write on the back of their *Character Sheets*. They might get additional information by overhearing other characters talking, trading clues, or blackmailing other characters. Students can also threaten to reveal other characters' secrets if the characters don't cough up information. Encourage students to improvise in making deals.

7. After previewing characters, have Inspector Jones read aloud the *Crime Scene Report*. When he is finished, post the report where students can reference it throughout the rest of the activity. Allow the remainder of the class period for students to mingle while gathering clues. This should be fun! Encourage students to role-play characters to the best of their ability, but monitor that students are acting appropriately. Also, encourage students to meet as many other characters as possible.

8. Students must also write answers to the four questions included on the *Crime Scene Report*. These questions can be collected and scored for completeness if you'd like.

9. After the party, have the students vote on the person they believe is the thief. Then, read the *Closure Read-Aloud* (page 159) to the students and finish with the *Habits of Mind Discussion* (page 174).

10. If you like, give students a character quiz, asking them to write short descriptions of at least eight characters they met.

Immigration, Industry, and the American Dream *(cont.)*

Things to Consider

1. Read the introduction and distribute *Character Sheets* the day before the actual mystery party. With some classes, you may have them some research additional facts about their characters, writing the facts on their *Character Sheets* as homework.

2. Margaret Carnegie is the culprit, though not a malicious one, as it turns out. Bela Lugosi is also involved in the crime. You will want strong students playing these roles, who will be able to keep the secret and avoid getting caught. You might even want to preview the roles with your chosen students before the mystery day.

3. The characters Thomas Bailey Aldrich and Inspector Jones will be asked to role-play prejudice against immigrants. Make sure you give these parts to students who can handle them appropriately.

4. Some of the *Character Sheets* are written at a fairly high reading level. With a younger class you may want to preview the characters and clues as a class discussion, or you can invite parents to join you for the day to help students as needed.

Introduction Read-Aloud

Welcome to the Party of the Century, held at the home of Mr. J.P. Morgan, one of the most successful businessmen of the Industrial Revolution! It's towards the end of 1900 and Andrew Carnegie has agreed to sell his company, Carnegie Steel, to J.P. Morgan for 480 million dollars. This deal would make J.P. Morgan's new company, U.S. Steel, the largest company in the world. It would be the first one worth more than one billion dollars.

It's at this party that Morgan will formally present Carnegie with the "Golden Key" that opens the bank vault where the $480 million is stored. At the start of the party, Carnegie and Morgan locked the golden key in an upstairs safe where it will stay until the presentation ceremony. But there's foul play afoot.

Everybody at the party has their own agenda, their own reasons for attending, their own secrets, and others' secrets they are keeping. And it seems like anybody who is anybody is here. There's Thomas Bailey Aldrich, who wrote a famous poem condemning immigration; Levi Strauss who immigrated to the U.S. but has already built up a huge jeans business in San Francisco; the bodybuilder Charles Atlas, who was born in Italy; and that creepy Bela Lugosi, who plays monsters in silent films.

We will role-play the Party of the Century, and who knows what could happen!

Immigration, Industry, and the American Dream *(cont.)*

Closure Read-Aloud

Though it was a splendid party, Bela Lugosi didn't feel like he quite fit in. In fact, there didn't seem to be any other Hungarian immigrants at the entire party. The only person he really got along with was little Margaret Carnegie. Though most kids were scared of Bela, he was kind at heart and loved showing off for children. And tonight he had a special trick.

Bela Lugosi had been sneaking around upstairs, when his abnormally large ears picked up the sound of J.P. Morgan's parrot talking to itself in the study. What was the parrot saying? Lugosi listened closer: "Five, forty-two, thirteen . . . five, forty-two, thirteen . . . squawk! Five, forty-two, . . . squawk!" It was the combination to the safe!

Lugosi knew better than to tell the combination to anyone at the party. It seemed as if there were more than a few people here who had reasons to steal the golden key, but he couldn't resist opening the safe just once. He brought Margaret Carnegie into the study, made a magician's spooky face, and spun the dials. Click! The safe popped open and Margaret clapped her little hands!

For Lugosi, that was the end of the night's adventure. He closed the safe and went back to the party. But, had he remembered to lock the safe behind him?

Margaret wanted another look at the pretty golden key. She told everyone at the party that she was tired and then snuck into the study. But, she was too short to reach the safe. Margaret was a resourceful girl and was happy to see all the books stacked neatly on their shelves. When she had been too short to play the piano, she had sat on two books, and now she pulled all the books off one of the low shelves and stacked them below the safe. The stack teetered back and forth, but Margaret was just able to grab the handle of the safe. It swung open easily and she snatched the golden key!

Margaret jumped off the stack of books and bumped into the side table with a loud bang. Oh, no! She was sure everyone would be mad if they saw her holding the key. She shoved the key in her pocket and ran to the bedroom at the end of the hall.

Not so long after this, Pien Ma, the Chinese butler was cleaning upstairs. Dusting was a regular part of his job and he knew that Mr. Morgan would want the safe especially shiny for tonight. But when Pien Ma dusted the handle of the safe, the door swung open. The golden key was gone! Pien Ma knew that because he was an immigrant, if he told people about the open safe and the missing key, they would accuse him of the crime. He quietly closed and locked the safe, and didn't tell anyone. Later in the night, after Inspector Jones and Thomas Bailey Aldrich accused him of the crime anyway, Pien Ma wished he had told the truth from the beginning, but by that point it was too late.

Did anyone in our class solve the crime?

Crime Scene Report

Directions: To be read aloud by Inspector Jones at the beginning of the party.

The most important event at this party is the presentation of the Golden Key. When J.P. Morgan gives the key to Andrew Carnegie, they will seal the deal to sell Carnegie Steel to Mr. Morgan for 480 million dollars.

Unfortunately, when Mr. Morgan goes to get the key from his upstairs wall safe, the key is missing! Here are the facts:

1. The safe was locked at the beginning of the party and it was locked when Mr. Morgan went to get the key at the end of the party.

2. The key was in the safe at the beginning of the party, and it's not there now.

3. There are many books lying around on the floor of the study where the wall safe is kept.

4. As far as you know now, there were no witnesses to the crime other than Mr. Morgan's pet bird.

As investigators, it's our job to answer four questions:

1. **How did the safe get unlocked?**

2. **Who stole the key and how did he or she do it?**

3. **Why did he or she steal the key?**

4. **Why did he or she relock the safe?**

Guest List

Andrew Carnegie—The owner of Carnegie Steel, Mr. Carnegie is a very rich man and today will become richer when he accepts the Golden Key from J.P. Morgan and seals the deal to sell Carnegie Steel for 480 million dollars.

Samuel Gompers—President of the American Federation of Labor, Mr. Gompers fights big business for the rights of workers.

Charles Atlas—Recently arrived from Italy, Mr. Atlas is a world-renowned body builder. He has difficulty carrying on a conversation without flexing.

J.P. Morgan—Mr. Morgan is a leader in the Industrial Revolution. He has been buying up many other companies and with this deal he will create U.S. Steel, the first company in the world worth more than one billion dollars.

Bela Lugosi—Most people think Mr. Lugosi should try harder to leave his famous monster characters in the movies. Mr. Lugosi frightens small children.

Levi Strauss—Though he has only been in the country a short while, Mr. Strauss has built quite a business selling jeans in San Francisco. He is very active in the Jewish immigrant community.

Lucy Parsons—A crusader for workers' rights, Ms. Parsons is a fiery union organizer and won't back down from a fight with big business.

Margaret Carnegie—Miss Carnegie is the six-year-old daughter of Andrew Carnegie. She's never been allowed to stay up this late before.

Inspector Jones—At such an important event, the inspector is there to ensure that everything goes smoothly, especially with all these suspicious immigrants around!

Father Edward Flanagan—Father Flanagan plans to emigrate from Ireland and started something called Boys Town, where struggling children and orphans can always find a home.

Pien Ma—Pien Ma is a butler in the Carnegie household. He originally came to this country from China as an indentured servant to work on the railroads out West.

Thomas Bailey Aldrich—He is the famous poet who wrote "Unguarded Gates," which many feel is unfair and mean to immigrants. Some people also agree with Mr. Aldrich.

Character Sheet: Andrew Carnegie

You were born in Scotland to a poor family, but after immigrating to the United States, you have achieved the American Dream! Through your own talents and hard work, you have become a very rich man. Your many factories manufacture steel, which you sell to railroads and to builders in the cities that seem to be springing up everywhere.

Though business is good, you are ready to sell your company to J.P. Morgan and spend the rest of your life giving your money away, mostly to libraries and universities. It is at this party that you will seal the deal. Once J.P. Morgan gives you the Golden Key, he will own your company (Carnegie Steel) and you will be 480 million dollars richer.

Though you have always tried to be fair to your workers, some people say you have made money at the expense of the "little person." Stick up for yourself when Samuel Gompers and Lucy Parsons attack your business practices!

Secrets you are trying to keep:

You think J.P. Morgan is arrogant and should give more of his money away to the poor. You are having second thoughts about selling your business to him. Don't let this information get out, or people might think you had something to do with the crime.

Secrets you know:

J.P. Morgan mumbles the safe combination out loud every time he opens it.

Questions to ask other characters: (Write their answers on the back of this page.)

Pien Ma: As a recent immigrant, do you ever feel discriminated against?

J.P. Morgan: What kind of bird is in the cage in your study?

Inspector Jones: How do you feel about the recent immigration wave?

Answers to other characters' questions:

1. Why are you selling your company to J.P. Morgan?

   I want to spend the rest of my life giving money away. I think the rich have a responsibility to give away most of their wealth.

2. Why would somebody steal the Golden Key from the safe?

   Either they wanted to steal the 480 million dollars, or they wanted to stop me from selling my company.

3. Who would want to stop the sale of your company?

   Mr. Gompers and Ms. Parsons hate big business and would love to see this deal stopped. Also, I think that Charles Atlas may have something to hide.

Character Sheet: Samuel Gompers

Sometimes businesses make money for their presidents by paying workers less money. Company presidents also make money by spending less on factory conditions. If workers can still make your products, who cares if the factory is dangerous?

As President of the American Federation of Labor, you make sure this doesn't happen! Don't let the big business leaders (Mr. Carnegie and Mr. Morgan) get away with paying their workers poor wages. You are a forceful and pushy person, who doesn't back down from a fight.

You are also an emigrant from England. Your parents were poor Russian Jews. Stick up for immigrant rights especially with Thomas Bailey Aldrich and Inspector Jones. Talk to Levi Strauss about his heritage. You both speak the Jewish language, Yiddish. When you talk to Strauss, you can pretend to speak another language.

Secrets you are trying to keep:

You and Ms. Parsons planned to steal the Golden Key and hold it hostage until Mr. Carnegie and Mr. Morgan agreed to make better conditions for workers in their factories. Don't let this information get out, or people might think you are guilty!

Secrets you know:

When you went to use the restroom, you saw Bela Lugosi sneaking down the stairs. Use this information however you like!

Questions to ask other characters: (Write their answers on the back of this page.)

J.P. Morgan: Why do you think all those books were spread around your floor?

Thomas Bailey Aldrich: Why did you write the poem "Unguarded Gates"?

Charles Atlas: Why did you come to America?

Answers to other characters' questions:

1. How do you know Lucy Parsons?

   We both help workers fight against big business for better working conditions. Not that we would do anything to stop the sale of Mr. Carnegie's company to Mr. Morgan.

2. What is the language you keep speaking with Levi Strauss?

   It's called Yiddish. We are both sons of Jewish immigrants. Why? Does it sound to you like we are planning something?

3. How do you feel about the deal between Carnegie and Morgan?

   I think its big business getting bigger, and I don't like it. These two have made their fortunes at the expense of the workers and it's time they paid for it.

Character Sheet: Charles Atlas

You are a recent emigrant from Italy and a famous bodybuilder. You can barely have a conversation without stopping to flex your bulging muscles and twirl your long mustache. Many people like Thomas Bailey Aldrich and Inspector Jones think of Italians immigrants as trash. Stick up for immigrant rights!

Secrets you are trying to keep:

You have saved enough money to return to Italy and plan to leave right after the party. Don't let this information get out, or it might look like you had already planned a quick escape!

Secrets you know:

You overheard Samuel Gompers and Lucy Parsons talking about stealing the Golden Key. Use this information however you like!

Questions to ask other characters: (Write their answers on the back of this page.)

Andrew Carnegie: Why are you selling your company to J.P. Morgan?

Bela Lugosi: Are you really a monster?

Pien Ma: How did you pay for your boat ticket from China to the United States?

Answers to other characters' questions:

1. Why did you come to America?

   I came to find the American Dream, but I never meant to stay. Like many Italian immigrants, I meant to earn money and return to Italy.

2. What is your job in the United States?

   I am a famous bodybuilder. Do you want to see me bend an iron bar across my back?

3. What is it like being an Italian immigrant in the United States?

   Most people think Italians are weak and stupid, but then I twist them into little pretzel shapes.

Character Sheet: J.P. Morgan

Though you started your career as an accountant, through your ambition and hard work you have achieved the American Dream! You are a very rich man. Once you give the Golden Key to Andrew Carnegie at this party, you will own his company (Carnegie Steel), and your own steel company (U.S. Steel) will be the world's first billion-dollar business.

You don't understand why Andrew Carnegie would decide to sell his business so that he could have more time to give his money away. While Carnegie gives money to build libraries, you would rather use your money to buy books for yourself. Your rare book collection is one of the finest in the world.

About the problem of immigration, you couldn't care less. Immigrants provide cheap labor. When Samuel Gompers and Lucy Parsons attack you about your business practices, stand up for yourself and tell them that at least your factories create jobs.

Secrets you are trying to keep:

Sometimes you say the combination to your safe out loud when you open it, though you're sure that no one has ever overheard you. You don't want this information to get out because it makes you look silly.

Secrets you know:

Inspector Jones and Thomas Bailey Aldrich are trying to frame your butler, Pien Ma, for the crime because he is a recent immigrant from China. Use this information however you like.

Questions to ask other characters: (Write their answers on the back of this page.)

Samuel Gompers: How do you know Lucy Parsons?

Inspector Jones: Who do you think committed the crime?

Lucy Parsons: Why don't you like me?

Answers to other characters' questions:

1. Who knew the combination to the safe?

   No one but myself. I guess I sometimes say the combination out loud as I spin the dials, but no one is ever around.

2. What kind of bird is in the cage in your study?

   It's a parrot. She repeats everything you say!

3. Why do you think all those books were spread around your floor?

   I don't know, but they were all taken from the lowest shelf, where I keep my collection of books by living authors. In fact, some of those authors are here tonight!

Character Sheet: Bela Lugosi

You live in Hungary and work in the growing film industry. You play scary monsters in silent movies. How does it feel to always play the movie monster? While you like your job, you're fed up with the discrimination that keeps anyone with an accent from playing the good guy. Stick up for immigrants' rights!

Secrets you are trying to keep:

Though you look pretty scary, you have always liked kids. You overheard Mr. Morgan's parrot saying the combination to the safe and unlocked it to show off for little Margaret Carnegie. You closed the safe, but you're not sure that you remembered to lock it. You might want to make a deal with Margaret Carnegie to make sure she stays quiet!

Secrets you know:

Margaret Carnegie didn't go straight to bed, because you saw her wandering around upstairs. Use this information however you like!

Questions to ask other characters: (Write their answers on the back of this page.)

Andrew Carnegie: Why would somebody steal the Golden Key from the safe?

Father Flanagan: Tell me about your plans for Boys Town.

Levi Strauss: What do you think about Inspector Jones?

Answers to other characters' questions:

1. Are you really a monster?

    No, I just play a scary monster in the movies. I'm actually really nice. Sometimes I can't help showing off for kids.

2. If you're not really a monster, why do you have such big ears?

    I can hear three times as well as most people. Right now I can even hear J.P. Morgan's bird talking!

3. Who do you suspect?

    It can't have been Margaret Carnegie unless she found a way to reach the safe. Maybe it was Pien Ma. He was upstairs by himself for awhile.

Character Sheet: Levi Strauss

You are a Jewish immigrant, who through your own hard work has achieved the American Dream. While you have gotten rich selling jeans in San Francisco, you still feel the weight of discrimination. You think that if it weren't for your Jewish heritage, you could be as successful as Carnegie or Morgan. Stick up for immigrant's rights!

Talk to Samuel Gompers about his heritage. You both speak the Jewish language Yiddish. When you talk to Gompers, you can pretend to speak another language.

Secrets you are trying to keep:

You spoke privately with Pien Ma upstairs and offered him a job working in your jeans factory out West. On the night of a crime it doesn't look good to be caught trying to steal servants from your host. Don't let this information get out or it might look like you had something to do with the crime!

Secrets you know:

In speaking with Samuel Gompers you found out that he and Lucy Parsons had planned to steal the Golden Key. Use this information however you like!

Questions to ask other characters: (Write their answers on the back of this page.)

Samuel Gompers: How do you feel about the deal between Carnegie and Morgan?

Bela Lugosi: If you're not really a monster, why do you have such big ears?

Father Flanagan: Did you know anyone at this party before tonight?

Answers to other characters' questions:

1. What do you think about Inspector Jones?

   I think he's prejudiced against immigrants and that he might be trying to frame someone without any real evidence just because he doesn't like him.

2. Why do you think your jeans company is so successful?

   Unlike other nationalities, most Jewish immigrants such as myself have always planned to stay in the United States. We built businesses to last instead of just looking for ways to make quick money to take home to our mother country.

3. What do you know about the books that were thrown around J.P. Morgan's floor?

   Many of the authors of those books are here tonight. Also, it looked like the books might not have been thrown. It looked like they might have been in a pile that tipped over.

Character Sheet: Lucy Parsons

Sometimes businesses make money for their presidents by paying workers less money. Company presidents (like J.P. Morgan) also make money by spending less on factory conditions. If workers still produce your products, who cares if the factory is dangerous? As an organizer for the workers unions, you don't let big business get away with this! If one worker speaks out against bad conditions, they get fired; but if all the workers get together in a union, the business can't fire them all without stopping production.

During a protest at Haymarket Square in support of an eight-hour workday, someone threw a bomb at police officers. Your husband was convicted for the crime and was hanged. You want to give J.P. Morgan and Andrew Carnegie a piece of your mind!

Secrets you are trying to keep:

You planned with Samuel Gompers to steal the Golden Key and to hold it ransom until Carnegie and Morgan agreed to create better conditions in their factories. Don't let this information get out or it might look like you had something to do with the crime!

Secrets you know:

You know that the Golden Key was stolen before Pien Ma went upstairs to clean. However, you might choose to blackmail Pien Ma anyway, just because you know that he was upstairs alone.

Questions to ask other characters: (Write their answers on the back of this page.)

Charles Atlas: What is your job in the United States?

Levi Strauss: What do you know about the books that were thrown around J.P. Morgan's floor?

Margaret Carnegie: What were you doing upstairs at the beginning of the party?

Answers to other characters' questions:

1. Why don't you like J.P. Morgan?

   My husband was hanged after throwing a bomb at policemen during a protest against big business. J.P. Morgan is just the kind of person we were protesting.

2. You are a union organizer, so what is a union?

   In a union, a group of workers get together to demand better working conditions or more pay. Unions make sure that businesses are being fair to their workers.

3. Why did you come to this party?

   Samuel Gompers and I came to the party to try to make J.P. Morgan treat the workers of U.S. Steel fairly.

Character Sheet: Margaret Carnegie

You are six years old and it's way past your bedtime. Your father, Andrew Carnegie, is a very rich man and tonight will become richer by selling his company (Carnegie Steel) to J.P. Morgan for 480 million dollars, but you don't see what is the big deal. This is the first big party you have been to, and the adults seem too busy to notice what you're up to most of the time.

Secrets you are trying to keep:

You are the thief! Don't tell anybody or the game will be ruined! Toward the beginning of the party, Bela Lugosi used the combination he heard from the parrot to open the safe (just showing off for you) but he left the safe door unlocked. You told everyone you were going to bed early and then stacked books under the safe until you could reach it. You wanted a closer look at the fabulous Golden Key and brought it back to your bedroom. You had planned to return the key, but then everyone went crazy about it being gone, and you didn't want to get in trouble! You might want to help Inspector Jones and Thomas Bailey Alrdich frame Pien Ma for the crime.

Secrets you know:

You were with Bela Lugosi when he used the combination he had heard from the parrot to open the safe. He closed the safe behind him, but he might have forgotten to lock it. Use this information however you want!

Questions to ask other characters: (Write their answers on the back of this page.)

Samuel Gompers: How do you know Lucy Parsons?

Charles Atlas: What is it like being an Italian immigrant in the United States?

Levi Strauss: Why do you think your jeans company is so successful?

Answers to other characters' questions:

1. What were you doing upstairs at the beginning of the party?

    Bela Lugosi invited me upstairs to show me a magic trick he had learned. He seems scary, but really he just loves to show off for children.

2. How can we be sure you aren't the thief?

    I didn't know the combination and even if I did, I'm too short to reach the safe.

3. Where have you been for most of the party?

    I got tired, so I went upstairs to take a nap in the guest bedroom.

Character Sheet: Inspector Jones

You are at the party to make sure that everything goes smoothly and it's a good thing you're here, with all these suspicious immigrants around. You don't like the look of Bela Lugosi, Levi Strauss, Charles Atlas, and Father Flannagan. You are especially suspicions of Pien Ma, who looks like he could steal something at any moment.

In your opinion, there are already few enough jobs in the United States without having to find work for the foreigners that keep showing up every day. You are outspoken about your beliefs and are not afraid to give these immigrants a piece of your mind! Stick up for the rights of the real Americans!

Secrets you are trying to keep:

You are working with Thomas Bailey Aldrich to frame Pien Ma for the crime because he is a recent Chinese immigrant. Your goal is to get people to vote for Pien Ma as the thief. Gather evidence and then convince people! You can even make up evidence, but don't get caught!

Secrets you know:

You know that Pien Ma found the safe unlocked while he was dusting upstairs and that the Golden Key had already been stolen. Use this information however you like!

Questions to ask other characters: (Write their answers on the back of this page.)

Andrew Carnegie: Who would want to stop the sale of your company?

Lucy Parsons: You are a union organizer, so what is a union?

Thomas Bailey Aldrich: Why do you think Pien Ma is the thief?

Answers to other characters' questions:

1. Who do you think committed the crime?

   It had to be an immigrant. Who else could be so dishonest, and who else here needed the money? I'll bet it was Pien Ma, the butler.

2. How do you feel about the recent immigration wave?

   I think that immigrants steal jobs that should go to real Americans.

Character Sheet: Father Edward Flanagan

You plan to immigrate to America in the next couple of years. Like many, you want to emigrate from Ireland to chase the American Dream. After reaching America you plan to start Boys Town, a home for orphans and troubled youths. You are a kindly old man, but through working with young hooligans you have learned not to take guff from anybody. Stick up for immigrant rights especially with Thomas Bailey Aldrich and Inspector Jones!

Secrets you are trying to keep:

Andrew Carnegie plans to donate money to help you start Boys Town, but you don't like J.P. Morgan. If it were up to you, Mr. Carnegie wouldn't sell his business to a man like Morgan. Don't let this information get out or people might think you had something to do with the crime!

Secrets you know:

A year ago Andrew Carnegie caught his daughter Margaret stealing and asked if you could help her. You don't think Margaret had anything to do with the crime, but you could use this information to blackmail her anyway!

Questions to ask other characters: (Write their answers on the back of this page.)

Bela Lugosi: Who do you suspect?

Margaret Carnegie: How can we be sure you aren't the thief?

Thomas Bailey Aldrich: Do you think your poem "Unguarded Gates" is fair to immigrants?

Answers to other characters' questions:

1. Tell me about your plans for Boys Town.

   I plan to start Boys Town as a place where troubled youths can always find a home. As an Irish immigrant, I will especially try to take care of wayward Irish youths.

2. Did you know anyone at this party before tonight?

   I had spoken with Andrew Carnegie about starting a girl's version of my Boys Town. I think maybe he has had some problems with his daughter.

Character Sheet: Pien Ma

You are a butler in the Carnegie household. Originally you came to the United States from China as an indentured servant, which means that someone paid for your ticket in exchange for you working as a slave for six years. Does this sound fair? Unlike the famous immigrants Charles Atlas, Bela Lugosi, Father Flanagan, and Levi Strauss, you can't speak out against people who display prejudice. You don't want to lose your job. You know that Inspector Jones is watching to see if you steal anything, and Thomas Bailey Aldrich keeps giving you dirty looks!

Secrets you are trying to keep:

You were upstairs dusting during the party and when you dusted the handle of the safe, the door swung open and the key had already been stolen! You locked the safe and didn't tell anybody because you knew they would never believe that you, a poor immigrant, had nothing to do with the theft.

Secrets you know:

When you were upstairs dusting, the books were stacked neatly below the safe. When you accidentally tipped over the stack, you panicked and ran from the room. What could those books have been doing there?

Questions to ask other characters: (Write their answers on the back of this page.)

J.P. Morgan: Who knew the combination to the safe?

Margaret Carnegie: Where have you been for most of the party?

Answers to other characters' questions:

1. How did you pay for your boat ticket from China to the United States?

    I came as an indentured servant, which means that someone paid for my ticket and in exchange, I worked without pay for this person for six years.

2. As a recent immigrant, do you ever feel discriminated against?

    Yes. I think most people don't trust immigrants. If I had important information, I might not tell anyone because they wouldn't believe me.

3. What were you doing upstairs toward the end of the party?

    I was dusting near the safe. But I swear I didn't steal the Golden Key!

Character Sheet: Thomas Bailey Aldrich

After being robbed, you wrote the poem "Unguarded Gates" about all the immigrants who keep showing up in the United States and making it unsafe for everyone who already lives here. In your poem you said, "My Americanism goes clean beyond yours. I believe in America for Americans." You don't like Charles Atlas, Bela Lugosi, Levi Strauss, and you especially don't like the butler, Pien Ma. All these immigrants are taking jobs that should go to real Americans!

Secrets you are trying to keep:

You are working with Inspector Jones to frame Pien Ma for the crime because he is a recent Chinese immigrant. Your goal is to get people to vote for Pien Ma as the thief. Gather evidence and then convince people! You can even make up evidence, but don't get caught!

Secrets you know:

Pien Ma didn't steal the Golden Key, but he did accidentally bump open the safe while he was upstairs dusting. The Golden Key was already gone!

Questions to ask other characters: (Write their answers on the back of this page.)

Samuel Gompers: What is the language you keep speaking with Levi Strauss?

Lucy Parsons: Why did you come to this party?

Pien Ma: What were you doing upstairs toward the end of the party?

Answers to other characters' questions:

1. Why did you write the poem "Unguarded Gates"?

   I had just been robbed. With all these immigrants coming to America, there's sure to be more crime and I wanted people to know about the dangers of immigration.

2. Do you think your poem "Unguarded Gates" is fair to immigrants?

   It may not be fair, but it's true. Immigrants like Pien Ma are to blame for most crime in this country.

3. Why do you think Pien Ma is the thief?

   Of all the immigrants at this party, the Chinese are the worst. That's why we need to stop all emigration from Asia.

Habits of Mind Discussion

1. Do you think this game was unfair to any of the characters?

2. Who in this game represented "industry"? What did your characters do?

3. Who represented "immigration"? Why did your characters come to this country and what was it like for them?

4. What is the American Dream? Who in this game had achieved the American Dream?

5. Do you think people still believe in the American Dream and do you think this dream is still possible?

6. Do people still immigrate to the United States, and do today's immigrants face any of the same challenges faced by immigrants in the early 1900s?

The Civil Rights Movement

Overview

Students will role-play museum curators and will explore African American art and music from before, during, and after the Harlem Renaissance. Through guided interaction with these artifacts students will experience the evolution of the African American artist from entertainer to respected member of the art community. Students will see how black pride and the Civil Rights Movement were born.

The total class time to complete the activity should be about two, 50-minute periods. You will measure student learning through discussion and evaluation of game activities.

Martin Luther King Jr.
Source: The Library of Congress

Objectives

- Students will identify and interpret examples of African American stereotyping and racism. (NCSS)
- Students will experience the way in which the development of African American art paralleled the awakening of the Civil Rights Movement.

Materials

- copies of reproducibles (pages 179–189) as described on page 176
- 9" x 12" envelopes to hold group packets
- scissors

The Civil Rights Movement *(cont.)*

Preparation

Total preparation time should be about 30 minutes. Ask a parent volunteer to help with the copying before you begin the activity.

1. Create a 9" x 12" envelope packet for each of the three groups. Each packet needs to contain the following:

   - a copy of the correct *Group Information Sheet* (pages 179–181)

   - *Artifact List* (page 182)

   - *African American Artifacts* (pages 183–186)

   - 3 copies of the *Fleming Model for Artifact Study* (pages 187–188)

2. Make an overhead transparency of the *Habits of Mind Discussion* (page 189) to use at the conclusion of the activity.

Directions

1. Split students into three groups. Each group will represent curators working on an exhibit of African American art from a specific time period (pre-1920, 1920–1945, and 1945–present). Read the *Introduction Read-Aloud* (page 177) to the students.

2. Distribute group packets containing the materials described above. After exploring their packets, groups will rank the artifacts on the *Artifacts List* 1–8 in order of the ones they most believe to be from their assigned time period.

3. Have each group choose three artifacts. Allow groups time to classify them according to the *Fleming Model for Artifact Study* (pages 187–188). Encourage groups to assign specific members to work on each of the top three artifacts they choose.

4. Once students are finished classifying their objects, ask them to discuss again whether they think the artifacts are appropriate to their time period. Give students time to classify any new artifacts, again using the *Fleming Model for Artifact Study* sheets.

5. Place artifacts in the space that represents your museum, with spaces labeled for each time period. At this point, if any artifacts are misclassified, place them in their correct periods.

6. Have groups present their artifacts to the class using the information they wrote on their Fleming model sheets, in chronological order. You may need to allow an appropriate amount of time for students to organize presentations.

7. Read the *Closure Read-Aloud* (page 178).

8. Close with the *Habits of Mind Discussion* (page 189).

The Civil Rights Movement *(cont.)*

Things to Consider

1. Group size is large compared to the other activities in this book; make sure all students are involved. You might want to grade students during the activity using one of the scoring guides included on pages 190–191 of this book.

2. This game depends less on role-playing and competition than many of the other activities in this book.

3. A few of the artifacts intentionally include depictions of racist attitudes. Make sure students are prepared for these images and are able to handle them appropriately.

Introduction Read-Aloud

It's almost time for the opening of the African American art exhibit at the [School Name] Museum. In fact, there are three exhibits, each from a slightly different time period, pre-1920, 1920–1945, and 1945–Present. Unfortunately, the crate with all the exhibit artifacts got jostled around in transit, and all the labels fell off. When the crate arrives, you can't tell which artifacts are supposed to go with which exhibits!

You will split into three groups of museum curators and will try to figure out which artifacts go with your time period. Your first step is to use your *Group Information Sheet* to figure out what life was like in during the time of your exhibit, and then rank on your *Artifact List* the artifacts from 1–8 depending on how sure you are that the artifact is yours. We will then be choosing artifacts and describing them using the *Fleming Model for Artifact Study* sheets. This is the same model that real curators use. After describing artifacts, we will be creating our classroom museum, and finally each group will get to present their artifacts to the rest of the class.

Good luck—make sure you get the right artifacts in your exhibit, or the public will be outraged!

The Civil Rights Movement (cont.)

Closure Read-Aloud

Even after the Harlem Renaissance, African Americans had to drink from separate fountains, go to separate schools, and had to sit in the back of public buses so that White people could have the better seats up front.

But, though the road to equality was still a long one, African Americans had started the wheels turning. By 1950, there were African American business owners, college graduates, and, of course, famous artists such as Jacob Lawrence who were respected all over the world. There were also black communities like Harlem where African Americans owned everything. Through the dangerous and hard work of Dr. Martin Luther King Jr., Rosa Parks, Malcolm X, Ruby Bridges, the leaders of the NAACP, and many, many others, African Americans were able to claim a piece of the phrase "all men are created equal." But even with these brave and committed leaders, equality didn't happen overnight; it was a process of many years in which not only laws but also long-held opinions had to change.

In fact, the struggle for civil rights isn't just something that happened in the past. This struggle continues today and isn't just a problem for African Americans. Any culture or way of thought can be a target for hate, and people still suffer under stereotypes. I'll bet that if you think carefully, most of you can come up with things you have heard, or maybe even things you have said without thinking, that put down a culture, religion, or race.

Answer Key to Artifact List

Pre-1920

Sheet Music: "Zip Coon"

Painting: The Banjo Lesson

Sheet Music: "Mr. Coon, You're All Right in Your Place"

1920–1945

Langston Hughes Poem: "Night Funeral in Harlem"

Drawing: Louis Armstrong

1945–Present:

Photograph: Mexico City Olympics

Photograph: March for Jobs

Photograph: Martin Luther King Jr.

Group Information Sheet: Pre-1920

Abraham Lincoln freed the slaves with the Emancipation Proclamation and the Thirteenth Amendment. However, African Americans are far from being truly "free." In the South, Jim Crow laws make sure that African Americans know their place. There are separate schools for white and black children and even segregated drinking fountains, swimming pools, and hotels. While African Americans are no longer slaves, they are paid such small wages that many owe money to their employers for housing and clothes. Until they can pay off their debts, they are not allowed to leave. How do you think this is different than slavery?

In white society, it is still popular to laugh at the comic idea of African Americans. Minstrel shows tour the country in which black Americans, or white people with black cork on their faces, pretend to be stupid and do things like steal chickens and eat watermelon. These stereotypes are accepted as truth.

Directions:

- Your first job is to look at the *Artifact List* and order the artifacts from 1–8. If you are sure the artifact belongs in your time period, order it close to 1.

- Describe your top three artifacts using the *Fleming Model for Artifact Study* sheets.

- After creating the classroom museum, you will be presenting your artifacts to the class. So, you need to prepare a brief presentation to share important information about each artifact. Be sure you include how and why it fits into your time period.

Group Information Sheet: 1920–1945

In this time period, for the first time, African Americans are starting to develop a sense of their own rights. Many have moved from the South, fleeing the strict Jim Crow laws and looking for a better life in northern cities. Especially in the area of New York City known as Harlem, African Americans are creating their own society. There are black shopkeepers and business owners, black teachers and policemen, and especially black artists. This period, known as the Harlem Renaissance (which means "rebirth"), sees African Americans moving from smiling entertainers who make fun of themselves for the amusement of the white world, to artists who create some of the world's best music, sculpture, and paintings. African Americans don't yet demand equal rights, but they are laying the groundwork of pride, education, and power that later generations will use to create the Civil Rights Movement.

Directions:

- Your first job is to look at the *Artifact List* and order the artifacts from 1–8. If you are sure the artifact belongs in your time period, order it close to 1.

- Describe your top three artifacts using the *Fleming Model for Artifact Study* sheets.

- After creating the classroom museum, you will be presenting your artifacts to the class. So, you need to prepare a brief presentation to share important information about each artifact. Be sure you include how and why it fits into your time period.

Group Information Sheet: 1945–Present

There are black shopkeepers and businessmen, professors, doctors, and artists. African Americans even fight for the country in World War II. It's getting harder for white America to justify a segregated country, with separate schools, hotels, and even drinking fountains. A strong black society filled with pride and power wakes up to demand equal rights. This is the period of the Civil Rights Movement.

In 1954, in a decision called *Brown vs. the Board of Education*, the Supreme Court said that schools could not be segregated and that black and white children would be equal. Many white people, especially in the South, fought this decision. African Americans had to stick together and stay strong. Much African American art from this time period shows black pride and strength.

Directions:

- Your first job is to look at the *Artifact List* and order the artifacts from 1–8. If you are sure the artifact belongs in your time period, order it close to 1.

- Describe your top three artifacts using the *Fleming Model for Artifact Study* sheets.

- After creating the classroom museum, you will be presenting your artifacts to the class. So, you need to prepare a brief presentation to share important information about each artifact. Be sure you include how and why it fits into your time period.

Artifact List

Direction: Discuss these artifacts as a group and rank them from 1–8 based on which ones you think are from your time period. Your top three (1–3) should be the ones you most think are from your time period. You will analyze these three artifacts further.

_____ **Sheet Music: "Zip Coon"**

The cover picture shows a well dressed African American with a huge smile.

_____ **Photograph: Mexico City Olympics**

Two black athletes stand on the podium without shoes, their gloved fists raised, and their heads bowed.

_____ **Sheet Music: "Mr. Coon, You're All Right in Your Place"**

Includes the words, "The Coroner said, there's another coon dead and that's all."

_____ **Drawing: Louis Armstrong**

Many people think of Louis Armstrong as the father of jazz.

_____ **Photograph: March for Jobs**

This photograph shows an African American girl holding a sign that says "March for Jobs."

_____ **Painting: The Banjo Lesson**

By Henry Tanner, this painting shows a poor grandfather and young boy.

_____ **Photograph: Martin Luther King Jr.**

Martin Luther King Jr. speaks to a large crowd of people.

_____ **Langston Hughes Poem: "Night Funeral in Harlem"**

This poem describes the culture of Harlem, New York.

African American Artifacts

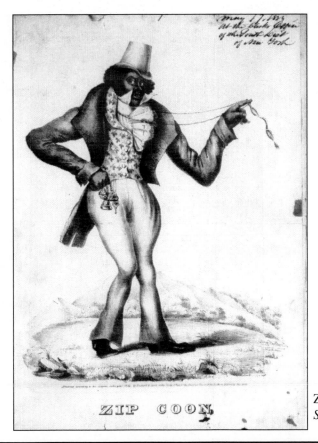

Zip Coon image
Source: The Library of Congress

Mr. Coon image
Source: The Library of Congress

African American Artifacts *(cont.)*

March for Jobs
Source: The Library of Congress

Night Funeral
In Harlem:

Who was it sent
That wreath of flowers?

Them flowers came
from that poor boy's friends—
They'll want flowers too,
When they meet their ends.

Night Funeral
In Harlem:

Who preached that
Black boy to his grave?

—An excerpt from a Langston Hughes poem "Night Funeral in Harlem"

African American Artifacts *(cont.)*

Black Pride at the Olympics
Source: Associated Press

African American Artifacts *(cont.)*

Martin Luther King Jr.
Source: The Library of Congress

The Banjo Lesson
Source: The National Archives

Fleming Model for Artifact Study

Name of Artifact_____

Identification

1. What materials would have been used to create the artifact?

   _____

   _____

   _____

2. What type of person do you think created the artifact?

   _____

   _____

3. Are there any interesting words or phrases on the artifact? If so, list them here.

   _____

   _____

   _____

   _____

4. How was this artifact used? What was its purpose?

   _____

   _____

   _____

   _____

Evaluation

5. Is the artifact one-of-a-kind or were many made just like this one?

   _____

   _____

   _____

Fleming Model for Artifact Study *(cont.)*

Cultural Analysis

6. Who would have used this artifact?

_____

_____

_____

_____

7. What else does the artifact tell you about the time period?

_____

_____

_____

_____

Interpretation

8. What could we use the artifact for in today's world?

_____

_____

_____

_____

9. What is the modern-day equivalent of the artifact?

_____

_____

_____

_____

Habits of Mind Discussion

- Why do you think African American pride was able to develop?

- What was the most important event in the Civil Rights Movement? Examples include the Emancipation Proclamation, *Brown vs. Board of Education*, Martin Luther King Jr.'s "I Have a Dream" speech, or Rosa Parks actions on her city bus.

- Do you think that racism still exists today? Can you give examples of racism?

- Does racism exist against groups other than African Americans?

Scoring Guides

Directions: Teachers can use this scoring guide and the one on the following page to assess independent student work.

Name _____   **Date** _____

5 Points	4 Points	3 Points	2 Points	1 Point
Student was productive, respectful, and collaborated well with others.	Student was productive and respectful.	Student completed works when reminded.	Student did not work well.	Student was interfering with others' work.

Teacher Comments:

Parent Signature:

Scoring Guides *(cont.)*

Name _____ Date _____

	Exceptional	Strong	Capable	Developing	Beginning	Emergent
	Student shows interest and enthusiasm; understands concepts and demonstrates learning; participates very well independently and in a group; produces high quality work on assignments; extends self beyond requirements; and uses a variety of resources.	Student shows interest and enthusiasm; demonstrates understanding of concepts; participates very well independently and in a group; produces high quality work on assignments; sometimes extends self beyond requirements; and sometimes uses additional resources.	Student shows interest; understands concepts; participates independently and in a group; and meets basic requirements.	Student shows interest occasionally; understands most concepts; participates infrequently; and sometimes meets basic requirements on assignments.	Student interest is not evident; understands some concepts; limited participation; and needs support to produce assignments.	Student shows little interest; understanding of concepts is limited; exerts minimal participation; and struggles to produce assignments.
	6 Points	**5 Points**	**4 Points**	**3 Points**	**2 Points**	**1 Point**

Description of Student Assignment

Teacher Comments:

Parent Signature:

About the Authors

Kristi Pikiewicz teaches language arts and social studies at Chief Joseph Middle School in Bozeman, Montana. A frequent presenter, she has worked with educators at numerous conferences in Montana and across the country. She spends much of her time helping educators learn to differentiate the learning in their classrooms. Ms. Pikiewicz has authored or co-authored a number of articles for teaching publications such as *History Matters* and *The National Council of Teachers of English Newsletter*. Having earned a bachelor's degree in environmental science, taught experiential science, and guided mountaineering for the Colorado Outward Bound School, Ms. Pikiewicz values hands-on, discovery-based learning in her classroom.

Garth Sundem is a full-time freelance writer with a background in music education. He graduated from Cornell University and earned a master's degree by studying composition with the jazz bassist Chuck Israels. Among other projects, he has composed for and conducted the Henry Mancini Orchestra in Los Angeles. Mr. Sundem's recent publications include articles for *Sea Kayaker*, *Adirondack Life*, *Cruising World*, *Veggie Life*, *Carve*, *Backhome*, *Music for the Love of It*, *Bozeman Outside*, and *Trail Runner*. He has taught language arts and music and has worked as a behavior specialist in the public schools. He continues to maintain a studio for private writing and music instruction.